THE CALIFORNIA GOLD RUSH

Also by Gordon V. Axon
The Stock Market Crash of 1929

GORDON V. AXON

THE

CALIFORNIA

GOLD RUSH

 MASON / CHARTER

NEW YORK 1976

1 2 3 4 5 6 7 8 9 10

Library of Congress Cataloging in Publication Data

Axon, Gordon V
  The California gold rush.

  Bibliography: p.
  Includes index.
  1. California—Gold discoveries. 2. California
—History—1846-1850. I. Title.
F865.A86   979.4′04   76-28339
ISBN 0-88405-367-9

CONTENTS

Introduction   1

I THE CALIFORNIA GOLD RUSH

1 California Drops Its Crock of Gold   5

2 South of the Border, Down Mexico Way   9

3 It Was Manifest Destiny   15

4 California Gold Before the Gold Rush   20

5 Eureka! Gold From the American River!   25

6 Those Happy Days of 1848   32

7 Oh, California, That's the Land for Me!   37

8 What the Forty-niners Left, and
  What They Found   46

9 Leave Town—or Else!   58

10 We Don't Like Your Looks!   66

11 The Ripples from the Rush   73

12 What Did the Gold Rush Achieve?   83

II FOR DISCUSSION

13 Was James K. Polk a Great President?   91

14 Was Manifest Destiny a Valid Moral Concept?   98

15 Why Did Some Nations Fear the Gold Rush?   104

16 Is Discrimination Ever Justified?   109

17 Suppose There Had Been No Gold Rush   114

    Appendix: The Lure of Gold   119

    Glossary   129

    Additional Reading   132

    Index   133

LIST OF ILLUSTRATIONS

Captain John Augustus Sutter   26

On Board the Panama Steamer   39

Seeing the Elephant   43

The Port of San Francisco in 1849   46

Mining in Teams   52

Hangtown in the Early Fifties   63

A Regular Gold Dustman   76

INTRODUCTION

It is the morning of Monday, January 24, 1848. At Coloma, about forty miles east of what is now the city of Sacramento, the workmen building John A. Sutter's water-driven sawmill prepare for another day, another week. Their boss, James W. Marshall, takes a stroll to look at the site, in particular to examine the tailrace, the small canal that discharges the water leaving the mill.

On the previous Friday, they had dammed the south fork of the American River, turning it over the new channel to the mill and the tailrace to sweep away the rubble of the excavations. As he looked around at the rushing waters, Marshall saw that the stream had done its work well. The site had been cleaned by the river. Part of the tailrace had been covered with silt.

Marshall glanced from the gravel bank to the dam, sizing up the job still to be done. His eyes moved back to the sawmill and the tailrace, on to the silt just where the tailrace entered the river.

As he looked up and down the course of the tailrace, Marshall caught something gleaming in the early morning sun.

He stared now, fixing his eyes on the spot, wondering if he could be seeing things. He walked rapidly to the gleams, scraped up some of the silt, and sorted it with his fingers.

Marshall stood there quietly, his heart pounding. For years he had heard tales of gold. Could these yellow flakes, these small golden peas, actually be gold? Or were they fool's gold, the yellow iron pyrite, worth nothing?

Marshall gathered up more silt and let the water swirl it away from his cupped hands. A few grains of heavy yellow metal were left in his palms. Marshall stared at them curiously, then looked again at the gravel bank formed by the rushing waters. He was sure he had found gold.

PART ONE

THE CALIFORNIA GOLD RUSH

CALIFORNIA DROPS ITS CROCK OF GOLD

Into what sort of world did California drop its crock of gold? Certainly not the world we know today and take for granted. No transcontinental railroad linked the Atlantic and Pacific coasts of the United States. California had been an isolated northerly province of Mexico until the Mexican War of 1846–1848 transformed it into an even more distant part of the United States. There was no Panama Canal. Most of the world did not even know where California was. When they finally learned that gold had been discovered in California, people simply asked, "California? Where's California?"

That land of gold was much less developed in 1848 than were the original thirteen colonies in 1776. Yet in 1850, California joined the other states in the Union. How could the golden spark of 1848 produce such a miracle?

The answer is to be found in the rapidly changing world. California was simply a sunny but sleepy Spanish-Mexican province with a non-Indian population of 14,000, dependent on cattle, hides, and tallow. Much of the rest of the world was seething with action. Politically, technologically, and socially, revolutions were occurring everywhere.

One of the most important, of course, had taken place in 1776 when the American colonies declared their independence of Britain. That act of splendid audacity had produced worldwide repercussions. The French soon had their own revolution. Spain and Portugal were shorn of most of their colonies within fifty years. Latin America turned into independent nations. Mexico, formerly part of New Spain, became an empire of its own, including within its massive territory distant sections, such as Texas, soon to be very much interested in declaring their own independence of Mexico.

Other nations also were changing. In Europe, 1848 was a year of revolution. Great Britain had escaped the turmoil, partly because its own industrialization was well advanced and partly because its discontented working classes had earlier received a few mites of social consolation.

Shortly after 1836, for instance, a financial crisis, bad harvests, and an economic depression had caused social anguish as factory workers tried to gain political power to achieve their ends. Long hours of work and high bread prices brought demands for change, just as earlier political agitation had produced the important Reform Bill of 1832.

The repeal in 1846 of the British corn laws (which included a tariff on wheat imports) had pleased the two most disgruntled elements of the population, the workers, who wanted a lower cost of living, and their employers, who demanded international free trade—that is, without tariffs—to improve their export markets. So Britain was relatively peaceful in early 1848 as revolution erupted in France, Germany, Italy, and the multinational Austrian Empire.

Other peoples were not so lucky. In Ireland, the "hungry forties" had begun. A fungus known as the Late Blight had savaged the potato crop from 1845 on. In the terrible famine years of 1845–1847, about half a million Irish died and a million emigrated.

Life was almost as bad on the continent of Europe. France lagged in industrialization and social and political change. A crop failure in 1846 caused a full-scale economic crisis that produced surprising political discontent. The constitutional monarchy of Louis Philippe was overthrown in February 1848, and Paris saw a few days of civil war that June.

Italy was in even worse shape. Garibaldi, the Italian patriot, had not yet unified the squabbling sections into a nation. Germany was still a confederation and lagged behind both Britain and France in industrial skills. The hard times of the "hungry forties" produced both widespread discontent and a major revolution in Germany in 1848.

Austria, then an empire less industrialized than any other European power except Russia, was mainly a peasant society with a small industrial base. At the other end of the world, China was undergoing a population explosion and considerable economic and social troubles.

In short, the world in 1848 was suffering from a variety of problems, including the change from agriculture to industry, and from undemocratic rule to popular elections. Yet such developments as the railroads, the telegraph, and steamships pulled the world together even as social and political demands rent many nations.

Who could blame the starving, the slum tenants, the adventurous, the politically oppressed, and the badly paid factory workers and farmhands for saying, each to himself, on hearing the news of rivers sparkling with gold, "This is it! This is what I've been waiting for. I don't know where California is, but the sooner I get there the better"?

Certainly not two refugees from the continent of Europe who were in London at the time, making ends meet by doing a spot of writing. Karl Marx and Friedrich Engels had their own views of society and expressed them in a pamphlet known as the *Communist Manifesto*, published in London in that banner year, 1848.

So off the goldbugs rushed, like so many lemmings to the sea. That is why, as Lord Bryce wrote, California grew "like a gourd in the night." That is how California was transformed, almost in the twinkling of an eye, from an underpopulated, undeveloped province of Mexico into a bustling, booming vigorous state that demanded and got entrance into the Union on September 9, 1850, without passing through territorial status.

Visions of gold sucked in tens of thousands from the ends of the earth. The fantastic and demonic drive of frenzied humanity to the distant goldfields of California was on. The "gold mania," as the London *Times* called it, had begun.

But we must first step back a bit and cast our eyes south of the border, down Mexico way, since the gold was discovered on what was then, in international law, Mexican land.

SOUTH OF THE BORDER, DOWN MEXICO WAY

The country now known as Mexico was earlier part of a vast area, called New Spain, that once also included the states of Florida, Texas, and California. Much of this huge territory had been conquered or claimed by Spain early in the sixteenth century, and for three hundred years had been part of the Spanish Empire.

Even though the last Indian empire in Mexico, that of the Aztecs, had produced a civilization of large cities, the Spaniards found their conquest easy. They took Mexico's wealth even as the indigenous Indians lived in poverty and subjection.

Changes in Spain itself, following the Age of Napoleon that ended with the Battle of Waterloo in 1815, frightened the conservatives across the Atlantic in New Spain. They feared that the liberal trend in Europe could easily cause them trouble. So they took advantage of Spain's domestic difficulties to declare their independence in 1821.

The new nation, known as the Mexican Empire, was itself so vast that some of the northern reaches, including what are now Texas and California, were far enough removed from the center of power in Mexico City that they considered themselves almost like overseas colonies—and began behaving like colonies seeking their independence.

By this time, of course, Americans were well on their way westward. Some 30,000 were in Texas by 1830. The trend was obvious. More and more Americans would settle in Texas, turning it into American-occupied territory. Mexicans, under President Santa Anna, hoped to solve the problem by preventing further settlement by Americans, but it was too late, and, in March 1836, Texas declared its independence of Mexico.

Mexico tried to turn the clock back militarily, and achieved an early victory at the Alamo, where Santa Anna wiped out the Texans. But this was followed by his total defeat, capture, and release. Texas became an independent republic under the Lone Star.

This did not entirely please the United States, since the feeling was growing that Americans were destined to settle much if not all of North America under one flag. The creation of independent republics such as Texas, after the model set in Latin America by the former Spanish and Portuguese colonies, could create problems.

Fortunately, Texas wished to join the Union, even though Mexico objected. By the American presidential election of 1844, the matter of annexing Texas was in the forefront of debate. The election of James K. Polk, Democrat, on an expansionist platform, meant trouble for Mexico, since Polk was determined not only to annex the independent Texas but also to claim another huge chunk of Mexican territory to the west of Texas, including what is now the state of California.

The Republic of Texas was annexed by the United States under President Polk in 1845. Mexico broke off diplomatic relations. The stage was set for the two-year war that began late in 1846, was fought mainly in 1847, and was settled on February 2, 1848, by the Treaty of Guadalupe Hidalgo. Mexico was forced to cede the northern third of its territory, including what is now California, but received financial compensation.

The American victory came just in time. Only nine days before the signing of the treaty, that is, on January 24, 1848, gold had been discovered in California—the gold that ultimately set off the California gold rush. Mexico could not have known about the gold, and could have done little or nothing about it had it known.

Until then, California had been a distant and sparsely populated province in the Mexican nation, but it had not been neglected by Americans, particularly Yankee traders from Boston, Massachusetts. Before 1840, the main interest was the fur trade, but the cattle-raising in California, and the resulting hide and tallow sales, were becoming more important. Many Yankees did a brisk business in the skins of the sea otter and beaver, hides, leather, and tallow.

Indeed, in 1840, Richard Henry Dana, Jr., had published his book *Two Years Before the Mast*, the story of his sea voyage to California and back in 1834–1836. The book was an instant international success, naturally drawing worldwide attention to California, even though its exact geographical position was seldom understood.

In 1841, California was visited by the first scientific expedition of its kind authorized by the Congress of the United States. This voyage around the South Seas was commanded by Lieutenant Charles Wilkes, U.S.N., later of Civil War fame, and included the famous mineralogist James Dwight Dana. By chance, one of the ships, the *Peacock,* was wrecked on the bar of the Columbia River in 1841. Dana with others journeyed on horseback from Fort Vancouver to San Francisco, following the Sacramento River from its source.

In this way, a New England mineralogist became one of the first Americans to visit in 1841 the general area, although not the exact spot, where gold was discovered in 1848. Dana, indeed, stayed with John A. Sutter, on whose property the gold was later discovered. Dana incidentally informed Sutter

11

in 1841 that the rocks in many parts of the area resembled the gold-bearing rocks in other regions.

California was obviously in many American minds long before the Mexican War. The attractions were numerous. Major migration to California began in 1841 when the first covered wagon train of settlers left Missouri. More and more Americans settled in California. Many played host on their ranches to Yankee traders. The news got back to Boston, New York, New Orleans, and elsewhere that life on the Pacific coast was open, free, and sunny.

The westward movement grew steadily. By 1844, Americans in California outnumbered Mexicans. What had happened in Texas a decade earlier began to happen in California: Americans thought of independence from Mexico.

Nothing could stop the drive to the west. The famous Donner Party, for instance, had set off in 1846 but reached the coast only in 1847 after a fearful experience, incredible sufferings, deaths, and cannibalism. It was from Sutter's solid settlement at New Helvetia that four expeditions were sent to aid the Donner Party, trapped in the snows of the high Sierra Nevada (Snowy Mountains). Sutter's was then the only outpost of civilization in the entire central valley.

More migrants followed in 1847 when the snows had melted and enough forage was available for the cattle. The news was out that California was a great place to be—in spite of the obstacles to getting there. From Independence, Missouri, and other places, immigrants made their way west. Some went via the Oregon Trail to the Pacific Northwest. Others took trails, and variants of old trails, into California to the south.

Increasingly, the news in the eastern United States concerned the Oregon Trail and California. More and more Americans felt the pull of the Pacific. They decided to dig up their roots and take the overland route to California, obstacles and all.

Even by early 1848, the opportunity to settle the land

called the Oregon country or California seemed to many almost too good to miss. The misfortunes of the Donner Party must have kept some back, but the major move west was well under way.

The capture of Mexico City by the American general Winfield Scott on September 14, 1847, the discovery of gold on January 24, 1848, in California, and the peace treaty with Mexico on February 2, 1848, came almost simultaneously.

At first, the golden news was not believed. It was just a Yankee trick, said some, to get people to settle there and make sure that Mexico could never get California back. But the news was insistent. The rumors became ever more fabulous. From specks of gold in the mud, talk was heard of nuggets of gold, then boulders of gold, then mountains of solid gold and rivers sparkling with gold. "Your streams have minnows in them, and ours are paved with gold!" cried one Californian.

The press printed the news. Eventually, the discovery of gold was reported in scientific journals. One of the first scientists to get the news was the same James Dana who had stayed with Sutter in 1841. In 1848, Dana was one of the editors of *The American Journal of Science and Arts*. In the November 1848 issue, on pages 270–71, there appeared a letter from the Rev. C. S. Lyman, dated Pueblo de San José, March 24, 1848. The letter mainly concerned the rich cinnabar (mercury or quicksilver) mines in upper California, but it also mentioned silver and coal. The last paragraph reads:

> Gold has been found recently on the Sacramento, near Sutter's Fort. It occurs in small masses in the sands of a new millrace, and is said to promise well.

The excitement mounted. More and more people believed what they were told. They began to think of going west. Others were already on their way. The trip out was difficult enough. Those roughing it over the prairies and the Rockies had much to contend with, including Indian attack, forage for animals, lack of fresh water and food, and the repair of wagons.

But there was something else, something that had long bothered the nation's leaders, thinkers, writers, and men of God. That was the taking of more and more land in the west. Could this be justified when the United States had so much land already? Was the United States destined to occupy land—all the land—beyond the Mississippi? Where were the moral grounds for such expansion? How could such a huge United States be governed?

Some Americans made no bones about the drive west. They welcomed it, believed it to be part and parcel of the nation's inheritance. Others were not so sure. They had misgivings, doubts, fears, moral qualms.

But necessity, as the proverb says, is the mother of invention. That is why, before going on to the California gold rush itself, we must examine the coining of a phrase that dominated American thinking for generations: Manifest Destiny.

3

IT WAS MANIFEST DESTINY

Americans themselves were on the move to the west coast long before the gold discovery, but only after 1840 did considerable numbers reach the Pacific. The "Oregon fever" then brought covered wagons to the area south of the Columbia River. Yankee shipping merchants, however, for years had swapped manufactured goods for hides and tallow with Mexicans on their ranches in California.

Thus the discovery of gold in California came at a very special time in the nation's history. The vast open spaces and the Pacific coast were attracting hundreds of Americans—yet these lands did not belong to the United States!

The moral dilemma facing the nation became obvious with the question of Texas, once part of the New Spain that later was known as Mexico when that country became independent of Spain in 1821. Texas had become independent of Mexico under the Lone Star flag in 1836, and wished to join the United States. But Texas was slave territory, and the question of slavery had become a grave national issue by the 1840s.

The presidential election of 1844 developed the growing debate between expansionism and anti-expansionism. By linking Texas with the Oregon country (a vast area compared with the present state of Oregon), to provide for free as well as for slave states, decisive action on the moral issue of slavery was temporarily avoided.

The election was narrowly won against Henry Clay, Whig, by the expansionist Democrat, James K. Polk of Tennessee, supported by southerners. Under Polk, Texas became a state in 1845, but Mexico objected, since it had never accepted the 1836 independence of Texas. The United States thus found itself in 1846 at war with Mexico just as the Oregon question with Great Britain was coming to a boil—since Britain ruled Canada, and Canada, like the United States, was expanding westward.

By 1845, therefore, the question of what land the United States was entitled to, and should seize, had become a matter for violent controversy. The question of international morality was raised.

The United States was in a very difficult position. It had become independent itself in 1776, and had encouraged other nations, such as those of Latin America, to declare their own independence of Spain and Portugal.

These declarations of independence were easily accepted by the United States where distant lands, such as Brazil and Bolivia, were concerned, but nearer home, as with Mexico, the matter was not so simple.

Mexico was on the American doorstep and an empire in its own right. It was entitled to its own independence and its own territory. But what if such lands included segments that wished to declare their independence of Mexico, as Texas did? Was Texas entitled to its own independence? Or must it become a state of the Union? And how about California?

The Oregon country was another moral problem for the United States. This area was prized by Canada, which was then ruled by Britain. Was the United States justified in insisting that all these problems be decided for its own benefit against Mexico and Canada?

What Americans needed badly by 1845 was some moral justification for taking the land they wanted. Otherwise, North America might become similar to South America— split up into many independent nations following the lines of Spanish and Portuguese colonial policy.

Obviously, an appeal to selfish national interests would not suffice, since all nations—Britain (Canada) and Mexico included—could claim the same rights. An appeal had to be made to a higher authority if Americans were to justify grabbing all the territory they wanted and still have an easy conscience.

Not surprisingly, the moral void was soon filled, in July 1845, just as President Polk, an expansionist, began the one-term presidency that added vast areas to the United States and settled finally the matter of the Oregon country, Mexico, and California.

The moral justification for expansionism came in two words: Manifest Destiny. The joining of "manifest" and "destiny" was the brainchild, or chance performance, of John L. O'Sullivan, a New York editor. In his own journal, then called *The United States Magazine and Democratic Review,* O'Sullivan carried one of his articles on the matter of annexation. He wrote that it was the nation's "manifest destiny to overspread the continent allotted by Providence for the free development of our yearly multiplying millions."

The original use of Manifest Destiny in the July 1845 article attracted no great attention, but the growing debate over Texas, the Oregon country, and the war with Mexico encouraged O'Sullivan to use the expression again, in December 1845 in the New York *Morning News,* to support the American claim to the Oregon country.

This time, the expression was seized upon by politicians and widely used nationally. It remains to this day in the national lexicon. The two words, "manifest" and "destiny," deserve closer study, since they were to appear and reappear thousands of times in the years ahead.

The words conjure up the divine inevitability of American expansion. The word "manifest" itself has biblical connotations. In a religious age, it rang of eternal truths. In an era not yet dominated by the biologist Charles Darwin or the economist Karl Marx, destiny was a preordained truth. The combination of the two words was a stroke of genius, even if unwitting, since "destiny" conjures up not just fortune or fate, but the inevitable succession of events. Who can resist the divine revelation of a nation's fate? Certainly not those itching for an excuse to cast off the shackles of doubt, the twitchings of conscience, the sense of greed.

The opportunity was obviously too good to be missed. Manifest Destiny caught the imagination of the people and became the excuse for almost everything connected with expansionism. The drive west acquired religious fervor. An aura of divine blessing graced the footsteps of those rushing hellbent for the Pacific. Two words had saved a nation's face.

Certain other countries were not impressed by this literary coinage. Mexico was one, Britain another. They were greatly concerned about American expansion—and for obvious reasons. Mexico was in the way in the south, and Britain's Canada in the north.

Both nations were directly affected by President Polk's four goals for his announced one-term presidency. These related to tariff reduction, the banking of federal funds in an independent Treasury instead of in private banks that could fail, the settlement of the Oregon country question with Britain, and the acquisition of California from a Mexico already shorn of Texas.

Polk achieved all four aims. Being more anxious to get California than a bigger slice of the Pacific Northwest, and feeling that he had enough on his plate with Mexico, Polk agreed with Britain to accept as the boundary line the 49th parallel, not the "54–40" line of latitude that the United States had claimed.

Mexico was soon defeated, but under President Polk's wise leadership, the United States merely took the northern third of that nation, not the whole. In this way, the shape of the continental United States was settled almost as it now appears. The contours certainly suggest a manifest destiny.

That is how California justifiably became part of the United States. In the decade of the "fabulous forties" much happened to this nation, most of it away from the settled areas in the East. People were to become entranced with the West, the Golden West, and Go West, Young Man.

But without Manifest Destiny and President Polk's determination to annex California, that state today might be independent, or still part of Mexico, or even British, French, or under the Soviet Union.

Under its own Bear Flag of 1846, California was indeed briefly independent. That itself indicated what was possible, though not probable. Who knows what might have happened if vast amounts of gold had been discovered in California in the days of Spanish control, or later, shortly after Mexican independence from Spain?

History produces oddities, coincidences, ironies. The Spaniards looted the gold of Latin America, but missed that in California. The Mexicans mined much in California, especially quicksilver, but regarded the province as more suitable for agriculture, for which, among many things, the Golden State now is famous.

Even more curious is the history of gold in California, since it had been discovered and used years before the famous find that generated the California gold rush—as we shall see in the next chapter.

CALIFORNIA GOLD BEFORE
THE GOLD RUSH

The gold discovery of 1848 came as no surprise to those acquainted with the facts of mining in northern Mexico. For years, small quantities of gold had been recovered in what is now California. Much of it was in tiny nuggets, flakes, or dust. Yankee traders operating from New England ports would send or take some home, mainly as a curiosity.

The American Indians probably knew about it for centuries, but had no use for gold. The Spanish missionaries could easily have become aware of gold in the middle of the eighteenth century. Certainly, gold was known to the Mexicans in control in Mexico City. California Governor Juan Bautista Alvarado used wedding rings of Californian gold in August 1839. It came from the San Fernando Valley, where more gold was discovered in 1842 by Francisco Lopez. A shipment of gold went from California to Boston via Honolulu in 1841. The young author of *Two Years Before the Mast*, Richard Henry Dana, told of specimens of gold having been obtained when he was in California on his trip of 1834–1836.

In those days, gold was often carried and sold in quills, since the gold was usually in dust form and obtainable only in small amounts. A large quill, that of a vulture or turkey buzzard, could hold three ounces or more in its hollow shaft. The quills, being translucent, were often graduated to show the quantity in them. The gold was kept in by a stopper.

Long before that famous day in 1848, California produced gold, silver, copper, quicksilver, lead, sulfur, coal, and asphaltum (mineral pitch or asphalt). The American Indians always said there were mines of many metals, but the Californians of Spanish-Mexican descent were far more interested in cattle than in searching the canyons for mineral wealth.

Exceptions there were, of course, but the ranches of California were famous long before metals hit the public eye. The first mineral of significance was cinnabar, the ore of mercury or quicksilver that is over 85 percent metal. This mineral was called "red earth" by the Indians, who used it to paint their bodies.

Some people did look for gold. One such was an old Canadian Frenchman called Baptiste Ruelle, who discovered gold in 1841 in what is now Los Angeles County. He had been a trapper for the Hudson's Bay Company. Like many other trappers, he became interested in the rocks he was accustomed to scrambling over, and became a miner. But his find was of small importance.

Of greater historical significance was the discovery by Francisco Lopez, usually described as a Mexican *vaquero,* or cowboy, who found gold in the San Fernando Valley on March 9, 1842, in a canyon, later called Placerita Canyon, about thirty-five to forty miles northwest of Los Angeles. This cowboy, who probably could better be described as a rancher, left home one morning to look after his cattle. Coming back, he remembered to pick some wild onions for his wife. When he saw particles of gold attached to the onion roots, he realized he had found the precious metal for which he had long patiently searched.

A modest local gold rush developed, and for years the area was worked and extended. Historically, this gold discovery is important for producing the first known significant quantities of gold. Talk of it spread and helped the growing interest in mining that became common after 1840. By that time, Mexico's control over its distant province of California was weakening, and more and more California residents of American origin were thinking that independence from Mexico would be a good thing.

Until then, the American Indians had been very secretive about gold deposits, and the padres of the Spanish missions had thought it best to keep what they knew quiet, especially since they often were at loggerheads with those running the show from Mexico City.

At first blush, the idea that gold could be discovered clinging to onion roots is a little hard to believe. Yet the forty-niners often did something very similar when they gathered grasses and washed the soil in a bucket of water, often recovering substantial quantities of gold.

Gold is usually found in very fine particles. Often it is called gold dust. Many rocks containing commercial quantities of gold show absolutely no trace of gold, even on close examination. But the gold becomes evident on panning—using water to swirl the gravel in a flattish, circular container. Nuggets, even boulders of gold have been found, of course, but most of the gold produced in the course of history has come from rocks that at first glance showed no evidence of gold.

This fact is borne out by the experience of the Scottish botanist David Douglas, who was in California in 1829–1832, and after whom the Douglas fir was named. He sent home numerous plants, including pines that later were found to have small flakes of gold held together in the clotted earth still attached to them.

Of greater interest, perhaps, is the question of just how much was known in Washington, D.C., by government officials, and later by President James K. Polk, about the mineral wealth of California. Apparently, they knew it was considerable. The first authentic shipment of Californian gold to a United States mint, that in Philadelphia, took place on November 22, 1842. The government clearly knew that gold was being found in California—gold and many other minerals.

That fact was proven when President Polk sent his fourth annual Message to the Congress on December 5, 1848. He confirmed the January 24, 1848, gold discovery and reaffirmed the importance of the mineral resources of California. We may reasonably assume that a steady stream of gold had been coming out of California for three decades or so before James W. Marshall caused the sensation at Coloma on January 24.

We also know that one of Polk's aims on assuming the presidency was the acquisition of California. Had he heard about the Mexican rancher Francisco Lopez and his wild onion roots? Was President Polk another goldbug, obsessed with getting as much gold as he could for the United States? Possibly, but it hardly matters, since President Polk would have wanted California, gold or no gold.

For the record, the official discovery of gold in any reasonable quantity in California should be credited to Francisco Lopez, who for years, along with many others, worked the original deposit and extended it. But that was only a modest deposit, discovered, of course, when California was part of independent Mexico. The find had immediately been reported to Mexico City, but the news had no great impact anywhere other than locally.

The January 24, 1848, discovery at Sutter's mill, however, made when Mexico had been defeated and just nine days before the signing of the peace treaty at the village of Guadalupe Hidalgo near Mexico City on February 2, 1848, was the historically significant discovery.

By that time, of course, news of the find by James Wilson Marshall was trickling down the foothills into the coastal settlements, soon to spread across the continent and all over the world. Everywhere, the reaction was the same. The news was initially ignored, being classed as a Yankee invention or regarded as yet another small gold deposit. Only when it was realized that a major deposit had indeed been discovered did San Francisco, then California, the United States, and finally the whole world take notice.

Even today, the gold rush of 1849 is the greatest gold rush of history, since it was the first and aroused the greatest emotions. But in that crucible formed by the massive granite fortress of the High Sierra there was more than gold. Had there been only gold, the impact of the discovery would have been short-lived.

But there were so many things: gold, freedom, equality, a new life of opportunity, the expanding frontier, personal gain, Manifest Destiny, a social revolution, and an end to the incubus of history. They were all there for the taking, even though the forty-niners might not have put their aims in these terms.

The generations that have passed enable us to see more easily why the California gold rush evoked such strong popular emotions. The energy released by the gold find represented far more than thoughts of immediate gain, even though these were uppermost in the minds of the forty-niners. Whether they knew it or not, they were rushing from the old to the new, from civilization to the still wide-open spaces, from drudgery to hope. The emotional worldwide reaction was clearly part of the general revolutionary aspirations finding vent in one way or another all over the world.

EUREKA! GOLD FROM THE AMERICAN RIVER!

Modern California dates from the moment on January 24, 1848, when James W. Marshall discovered gold in the tailrace of the sawmill he was building at Coloma for John Augustus Sutter. Even before that historic day, of course, California had become the dream of many in the East. Sutter, who had lived in California for many years by 1848, realized that more and more Americans would settle there. He sensed that he would need increasing supplies of lumber for his building operations. So he asked his millwright, James Marshall, to locate and build a sawmill, powered, of course, by water. That is how gold came to be discovered.

Sutter was Swiss, born in 1803. He studied at a military college, and rose to the rank of captain in the French army. When he was thirty, Sutter and some of his friends and relations decided that the United States offered opportunities for vine growing. Sutter was chosen to find a suitable area for the project.

Sutter got as far as Missouri, found a place for the new settlement, and, with ample funds, bought the necessary stores and implements to make a start. But misfortune struck when

John Augustus Sutter, on whose property gold was discovered in January 1848. *Courtesy Title Insurance and Trust Company (Los Angeles) Collection of Historical Photographs.*

the Mississippi steamboat on which the stores had been loaded struck a snag and sank, a total loss.

Sutter stayed in the New World, however, had numerous adventures, and finally arrived in San Francisco. He then went up the Sacramento River and built a stockade, known as Sutter's Fort, now within the city limits of Sacramento. Sutter, who had received a land grant from Mexico, then the rulers of California, named the colony New Helvetia in honor of his native Switzerland, which had been called Helvetia in ancient times.

Captain Sutter soon became quite famous in the area. New Helvetia attracted numerous settlers and American Indians. The land was tilled, much wheat was grown and ground into flour, and furs were bought from trappers and hunters.

The United States war against Mexico left Captain Sutter in the catbird seat. The vast estate acquired from Mexico was now much more valuable. The Cap'n, as Sutter was known locally, was a man to be reckoned with, owning thousands of cattle, horses, mules, sheep, and hogs. His business was growing as more and more emigrants were coming to California. The Cap'n decided to get on with the job of building a sawmill that had been put off by the Mexican War. That decision was to affect the lives of millions.

Sutter had decided to use the trees in the foothills of the Sierra, and the rushing streams, to produce his own lumber instead of having expensive redwood brought up the Sacramento River from San Francisco. He needed plenty of sugar pine and a suitable stream, one powerful enough to work a sawmill and big enough to raft the lumber down to New Helvetia, but so situated that the sawmill would not be swept away by spring floods or sudden downpours.

James Wilson Marshall was the man Sutter selected to find a suitable site. Marshall was born in New Jersey in 1812. When he reached the age of twenty-one, he picked up stakes and moved west, staying in one place and another, finally ending up in Sutter's Fort working for Sutter.

The site Marshall picked in 1847, after he had served a stint in 1846 in the local Bear Flag War, was at Coloma on the American River. Coloma, from the Indian word *culluma*, meaning beautiful vale, was about thirty-five miles east of the fort as the crow flies, but some forty-five miles by horseback.

By early 1848, much of the work on the sawmill was done and Marshall and his men began building the tailrace, the small canal that discharges the water leaving the mill. The hard rock had to be blasted and the channel dug. To get rid of the debris, Marshall would turn the stream over the tailrace to sweep away the rubble overnight. In the morning, he would look around to inspect the progress and decide on the day's operations.

On Monday, January 24, 1848, Marshall as usual went to the sawmill to inspect the tailrace. The weekend was over, another week's work lay ahead. The river had swept away the rocks and rubble, covering part of the tailrace with silt. That's how Marshall came to see yellow particles in the dirt. Quite by chance, Marshall had used a method of gold mining later to become common in the California gold diggings. The stream itself provided the water for gold panning, with the stream bed acting as a huge pan or long tom. In short, it was panning on a mass-production basis.

Marshall collected some of the fine gold and took it with him. By January 28, Sutter in New Helvetia had been told about it, had tested the small yellow particles, and was satisfied they were gold. The secret was soon out. Some of the men working for Marshall at the sawmill and tailrace did some prospecting on their own. More gold was found. The news trickled down to San Francisco that gold had been found on the American River.

The first press account appeared on the last page of the San Francisco *Californian* for March 15. Few people noticed, or cared. On March 18, the *California Star* reported the find, and on March 25 the same newspaper noted that enough gold was being mined to make it "an article of traffic" at Sutter's Fort, New Helvetia. The *Star's* next issue, that of April 1, ran a story on California's prospects. Gold was mentioned, but the new find was lumped with the old one near Los Angeles. Over a month later, on May 6, gold was again mentioned, along with silver, but the emphasis as usual was on the streams, the trees, the crops, and the forage available for the main business of cattle-raising. Over three months had passed since the discovery of gold—and few people cared!

The reason is clear. California in 1848 was still sleepy. Only some 2,000 Americans lived there. It was still predominantly Spanish-Mexican and American Indian. The larger settlements were in the south, since most of the residents had come up from Mexico. The more northerly places such as San Francisco were much smaller. In June 1847, for instance, San Francisco boasted a population of 459, including 375 whites. A year later, those figures had roughly doubled. Even so, San Francisco with a population of some 800 could not have been too interested in gold reports seeping down from the foothills.

But the rumors kept coming. They did not die away. And the size of the gold finds grew. Instead of small gold washings, news spread of nuggets, big nuggets. A few souls in San Francisco decided to look for themselves. Spring had come. A trip into the hills would be refreshing.

Samuel Brannan, a Mormon elder and the head of a large party of Mormon emigrants who had reached California in 1846, was one who went. He soon discovered the truth, collected the tithes from the Mormons who had started their own diggings, and rushed back to San Francisco with the gold in a quinine bottle.

Brannan was so excited that he rushed about San Francisco shouting in his bullhorn voice: "Gold, gold! Gold from the American River!"

The effect was electric. People stared at the quinine bottle, heavy with gold, decided to do something about it, then dashed off. Soon all San Francisco knew. A mad rush to the hills developed. Sailors left their ships and skedaddled. Within days of Brannan's bellowing like a bull on May 29, 1848, San Francisco had been deserted by most of its male population.

The word spread up and down the coast that fortunes were being made in gold. The soldiers in the garrison at Monterey simply got up and left. The U.S. military governor there, Colonel Richard B. Mason, and his adjutant, Lieutenant William T. Sherman, later of Civil war fame, wondered what to do about it—and decided to go and look for themselves.

In June and July, Mason and Sherman visited the mines, bought a quantity of gold, and sent it with a report to their superiors in Washington, D.C., where it ultimately reached President James K. Polk. The gold, in a tea caddy, weighed over 230 ounces and had been collected from various diggings. The report, dated August 17, 1848, was sent by Colonel Mason to Brigadier General R. Jones, Adjutant General U.S. Army, Washington, D.C.

President Polk was convinced. So were others. On December 5, 1848, Polk in his fourth annual Message to the Congress referred to the "rich and extensive territorial possessions" of New Mexico and California. In a specific reference to California's gold, Polk wrote:

It was known that mines of the precious metals existed to a considerable extent in California at the time of its acquisition. Recent discoveries render it probable that these mines are more extensive and valuable than was anticipated. The accounts of the abundance of gold in that territory are of such an extraordinary character as would scarcely command belief were they not corroborated by the authentic reports of officers in the public service who visited the mineral district and derived the facts which they detail from personal observation. Reluctant to credit the reports in general circulation as to the quantity of gold, the officer commanding our forces in California visited the mineral district in July last for the purpose of obtaining accurate information on the subject. His report to the War Department of the result of his examination and the facts obtained on the spot is herewith laid before Congress. When he visited the country there were about 4,000 persons engaged in collecting gold. There is every reason to believe that the number of persons so employed has since been augmented. The explorations already made warrant the belief that the supply is very large and that gold is found at various places in an extensive district of country.

The President's message made other references, such as to the mines of quicksilver ore, "believed to be among the most productive in the world," and to "this abundance of gold." His word reached the world at the same time that letters from Americans in California, telling of the gold discovery and local gold rush, were receiving wide publicity in this country and abroad.

The *New York Herald,* for instance, published a small item on California gold as early as August 19, 1848, but it received little attention. By this time, of course, the news from California had spread across the Pacific to what is now Hawaii. The word had gone north to the former Oregon country and south to Los Angeles, San Diego, and into Mexico. Ships sailing from San Francisco had taken the golden news into ports of call, such as Paita in Peru, and Valparaiso, Chile.

Already, gold seekers from Mexico, Hawaii, Chile, Peru, and other Pacific lands and islands were en route to California. They were soon to be joined by tens of thousands from New York, New Jersey, the New England states, the plains states, and nations all over the globe. The unbelievable had happened. Fortunes were being made, just by picking up gold! By December 1848, the youth of the world was on the move, headed for San Francisco. The stampede was on.

THOSE HAPPY DAYS OF 1848

Yes, the doubting Thomases believed President Polk's report of abundant gold in California. A mania swept the world. History records what happened. Almost forgotten in all the excitement are the forty-eighters, those Californians who were on the spot, or nearly so, as the news of the January 24 discovery made its way down the hills and valleys of the Sierra foothills, along the coastal settlements north and south of San Francisco, and into the incredulous world. Some of them later complained bitterly of the newcomers, the world's forty-niners, and longed for the good old days of 1848.

Small wonder, since they then had California all to themselves. These forty-eighters were few and far between in the vast area of northern Mexico—which is how many of them regarded it. Even by late 1845, California probably had only some 700 United States residents. By February 1848, their number had trebled to about 2,000. Keeping track of later developments is difficult, since California by then was United States territory. Immigration was stimulated by that, and, of course, by gold.

More American citizens were arriving all the time, some

after surviving incredible hardships as they crossed the Great Plains and the Rocky Mountains. But they were going to California, in those halcyon early days, to settle permanently, not to pick up a fortune in gold, then go back home.

Life in California was easygoing in the spring and summer of 1848, before the goldbugs arrived. The population was mainly American Indian or of Spanish and Mexican descent, with some Americans. They lived in San Diego, Los Angeles, Monterey, and San Francisco, small places, to be sure, by today's standards, and in the many even smaller settlements along the coast and hidden in the valleys. A trickle of new settlers entered California by sea, while others came up from Mexico, along the coast, or over the Rockies.

Life was peaceful—or so it seemed in retrospect. Suddenly, gold was discovered. So what? shrugged the old timers. We can almost hear them saying, "Big deal! Gold was discovered here years ago. We didn't come for gold. There's more to California than gold," then going back to their ranches and their cattle.

But when the richness of the gold find was confirmed, many of them had second thoughts. The better weather had arrived. It was no longer bitterly cold up in them thar hills, so off they went, to camp for a summer and to try their luck panning for gold.

Such were the men of forty-eight. They had ranches, businesses, or jobs, homes and families. They got the news of the gold in the spring and summer and went up into the hills, often with their families, camping out and having a good time.

They were joined, of course, by some who were in California by chance, such as sailors in the ports, and soldiers on duty or getting ready to go back east. Remember, the war against Mexico was only just over.

The spring, summer, and fall of 1848 saw much fun and excitement at the gold diggings. The stakes of the forty-eighters were not as high as those of the forty-niners, who

33

traveled far, risked much, and wished to get as much gold as they could. If the forty-eighters struck it lucky, fine; if not, well, it was just too bad. They simply went back to what they had been doing before, working in settlements along the coast, raising cattle, trading hides and tallow, or as farmers, mechanics or merchants.

So we must draw a distinction between the goldbugs of 1848 on the one hand, Californians of Indian, Spanish, Mexican, and American heritage who had settled there for reasons other than gold, and those of 1849 on the other hand, from Britain, Ireland, Germany, China, Australia, Peru, Bolivia, and many other lands, who went to California solely for gold.

Even so, the earlier goldbugs took advantage of the same conditions that brought the later ones: gold and free territory. Much of the land was, for all practical purposes, there for the taking, gold and all, even though some had been converted into huge estates, granted first by Spain and later by Mexico.

Especially important was the system of free mining. The absence of laws on mining in the Californian wilderness left it up to the gold miners, the diggers, to make their own. Local regulations were drawn up and widely accepted. No license was needed. There was no taxation. In short, you kept what you grabbed if it was free when you grabbed it. What other system could work in a land that up to a few months earlier had been Mexican territory, and was, in effect, without any organized local governments or system of justice?

Placer mines, or deposits of sand, gravel, or earth in the bed of a stream, provided most of the gold in 1848. The rules adopted gave right of ownership to those who had discovered the gold and were in possession of the deposit. In the case of gold-bearing lodes, or veins, often of quartz, in rock, ownership was attached to the vein itself. The person who found the vein, often several closely spaced veins running together as a unit, was the owner of the mine. If the vein extended beyond the limits of his claim, the owner had the right to

34

follow the vein wherever it led. (The word "lode" derives from the verb to lead.) Whatever the miner could follow, expecting to find still payable ore, was his for the taking, even though he had overrun into another miner's claim.

Obviously, these rules were adopted because they had the morality and practicality of the old adage, "First come, first served." Thus a miner finding a payable alluvial deposit, or placer, owned it as long as he stayed there. A digger who first spotted a gold-bearing vein of quartz owned the vein itself, even when it went beyond his claim.

These regulations favored not only the early birds, however, but the unscrupulous. That mattered less in the spring and summer of 1848, when many of the miners were simply having a lark, camping in the hills with their families, than later, when thousands of goldbugs were stalking the ravines and gullies, looking for sites not already taken.

Often these newcomers were lean and hungry men, desperate, sometimes armed. Rules, they argued, were meant to be broken. A few strong-arm tactics often worked miracles— especially against miners with nonwhite skins, those who spoke a foreign tongue or had greasy hair, the clannish, the foreigners, and any who did not wear the true garb, the red flannel shirt, of a real, true-blue American.

From the beginning, of course, the mining camps had to enforce rules of behavior. That was usually done on Sundays, everybody's day off. From the simple necessity of having to live by some rules of acceptable conduct, there developed the vigilantism that erupted in San Francisco in 1851 and in even worse form in 1856.

The summer of 1848 saw the beginnings of California's transformation. San Francisco lurched into world fame. The gold diggings slowly but surely changed their easygoing nature. The cooler weather arrived. Many of the local residents went back down the hills to their old jobs. They were replaced—more than replaced—by those arriving solely for gold.

Shrewd traders in Boston, New York, Philadelphia, Baltimore, and New Orleans had gotten wind of what was happening. They were digging out supplies of hard-to-sell items, spades and picks, medicine chests, food and clothing, and rushing them to San Francisco. Old tubs of freighters were hammered together and given a lick of fresh paint. Many foundered as they rounded Cape Horn. As we shall see, there wasn't any Panama Canal in those days. Whalers out of Boston were polished up and turned into passenger ships for the long haul to Eldorado, the place of gold.

The happy days of California's summer of 1848 were fading fast. The picnics were over. Digging for gold was becoming a very serious business indeed.

The newcomers of 1849 were right in thinking there was gold in California. They may have realized that many of the easy pickings had already gone, that much land had already been grabbed. They may also have suspected, and rightly, that the great mining years lay ahead.

But the forty-niners could hardly have believed they were destined to flourish as a romantic movement for but a few years, and that even those years would be, for most of them, full of hard toil. Few of them dreamed that within a short time they would be back at a job, working for others—this time for the men with money and with massive mining equipment that would quickly replace not only the solitary miner with his pan, but also the groups that banded together for self-protection, working their cradles, long toms, and sluices to keep skin and bones together as the days of the easy pickings faded into memory.

They could not have foreseen that, in Eldorado, they would come face to face with desperadoes for whom slitting a throat and pushing a body over a cliff were all in a day's, or a night's, work.

OH, CALIFORNIA,
THAT'S THE LAND FOR ME!

Meanwhile, of course, what mattered were dreams of gold, visions of a future free from drudgery, and the fervent belief in the good life in the sunshine. By late 1848 or early 1849, much of the world truly believed that gold had indeed been discovered in California and that fortunes were to be had for the picking. The news fired the imagination of thousands from San Francisco to China, from the Golden Gate to the harbor of New York, and from New York across the Atlantic to the struggling masses of Europe. Vast multitudes prepared to descend on the new Promised Land.

Discussions raged on how best to get to California. Those living west of San Francisco simply sailed out from China, Australia, New Zealand, and the islands of the Pacific. Those from Peru and Bolivia also found their way easily to the gold-fields.

Others had little or no choice. Emigrants living in states such as Iowa, Indiana, or Illinois had to go overland, especially if their assets were in cattle and farm equipment. New Yorkers, New Englanders, and Europeans had a choice of routes.

Three main ones existed. The shortest was overland across the continent of North America. A longer route was via the

Isthmus of Panama, then without a railroad or a canal. The longest way was around Cape Horn, the southernmost tip of South America.

The overland route had northerly trails, southerly trails, and various passes over the Sierra into California. The trip, by horse and covered wagon, was arduous. Mud and dust were nuisances. The dry air caused wagon wheels to fall off, and it was usually difficult to find wood for repairs. Food was sometimes scarce. Pure water was often at a premium. Tales of cannibalism were not uncommon. Some of the short cuts proved false and risky. There were fights with American Indians.

The Panama route also posed many problems. Emigrants had to get to Chagres, a small port on the Caribbean, cross the isthmus to the town of Panama, then go via the Pacific to San Francisco. The major trouble here was landing at Chagres, often by surf boat, going up the Chagres River in a native boat called a *bungo,* then walking or riding a mule across the low continental divide to Panama.

Chagres was described as a wet, dirty, hot, unhealthy town. It was a hellhole for many. On the thresholds of the doors, and in the huts, were thrown hides, bullocks' heads, fish, cattle, and other animals that putrefied in the damp tropical atmosphere. Part of this mess was used as food.

Gnats, mosquitoes, and ants bit and nipped away at gold seekers as they traveled from Chagres to Panama. Cholera and yellow fever were epidemic, especially in the rainy season, and dysentery and typhoid fever were also common.

Panama, an old Spanish town, was relatively pleasant. Those waiting for a passage to San Francisco could enjoy strolling through the sunny streets, looking at quaint churches and houses, visiting cockfights and bullfights, discovering monkeys and bananas, listening to strolling musicians, and taking life as it came until a berth was available.

Going via Cape Horn, was, of course, a long and tedious voyage. It was popular among gamblers and others who could put their time at sea to good use. The trip became

Panama became the crossroads for passengers en route to and from California. On the steamers, crowded conditions were the norm. *Courtesy Wells Fargo Bank History Room, San Francisco.*

known as the white-collar route, partly because it was favored by that type of emigrant, and partly because the lack of exercise produced many flabby males.

Usually, the clippers rounding the Cape from New York would stop in at prosperous Valparaiso in Chile. Other ports of call were Paita in Peru, and Panama. A few ships ventured off the beaten track. Some dropped anchor at the island immortalized in *Robinson Crusoe*, taking on wood, fruit, and water. Others called at the Galápagos Islands, now famous for the 1835 visit there by the good ship *Beagle*, which carried the British naturalist Charles Darwin.

There, both crew and passengers took time out from the gold rush to collect dozens of monster tortoises, which later would be turned into choice turtle soup. (Galápagos is Spanish for freshwater tortoises.)

Most of the voyagers, of course, were far more interested in gold than in Robinson Crusoe and giant tortoises, so they hastened to San Francisco as fast as possible, and with only those delays that were absolutely necessary.

Variants of the three major routes also came into use. Some emigrants sailed from New Orleans to Vera Cruz in Mexico, then crossed Mexico to Acapulco, and sailed to Eldorado from Acapulco. Some gold seekers crossed from the Atlantic to the Pacific by way of Nicaragua.

What strikes us today is the fantastic effort and the incredible risks run by many of those who rushed to seek gold in California. Then, the expense of the trip, the dangers, and the difficulties all were taken for granted. Today, it all seems unreal, even preposterous.

But the gold fever was abroad in the world. Perhaps "mania" is a better word for the state of mind that possessed tens of thousands of people. Most of the emigrants had never traveled before. Yet off they went, traveling thousands of miles, risking life and limb, for California gold.

How many perished on the way we shall never know. How many were killed by Indians, cholera, or typhus, or died from foul water or rotten beef? How many were shipwrecked as they rounded the Horn? How many bones rotted in the luxuriant vegetation of the Chagres River and the Isthmus of Panama? What numbers were lost in the Sierra, in Death Valley, and by the salt flats of Utah?

Thousands must have disappeared never to be heard from again. Many more thousands, of course, arrived in California as part of one of the greatest of human migrations.

It was that and more. For many goldbugs it became in retrospect the highlight of a drab life. For millions in political and economic chains, the California gold rush symbolized the end of poverty and oppression, the hope for a new life in the New World. So intense were the emotions and passions of the gold rush that songs were still being written about it decades after it was over. "Oh My Darling Clementine" was written in 1884 as a college song, yet is often regarded as a song of the forty-niners.

Yes, the forty-niners sang as they sailed. They sang with the boatmen as they crossed the Isthmus of Panama. They sang as they sighted San Francisco. They sang when they got back home—often penniless. They borrowed favorite tunes and prepared their own words to suit their taste. Many of the songs written just for the gold rush are now forgotten, but others linger on in golden memory.

The first gold-rush song shows how quickly the news of the 1848 discovery stimulated New England emigration to the new Eldorado. In November 1848, John Nichols, bound for San Francisco on the bark *Eliza*, wrote the words of "Oh, California" to the then very popular tune of Stephen C. Foster's "Oh! Susanna." The new chorus went:

> Oh, California,
> That's the land for me!
> I'm bound for San Francisco
> With my washbowl on my knee.

It caught on quickly, becoming a national anthem of the forty-niners. The words were changed to suit local persons, methods of going to California, and circumstances generally, but the melody remained Foster's, borrowed for the occasion.

The first gold-rush song written in California used the old American saying, "Seeing the Elephant," an expression meaning having seen enough, or more than enough. It was penned by David G. Robinson, a showman from New England.

Song writing became for the forty-niners almost as much a craze as the gold rush itself. All sorts of lyrics cropped up from nowhere and were used in all sorts of songs. One song ended with the chorus, "John I. Sherwood, he's a-going home." Nobody seemed to know who Sherwood was or why he was going home, but the song was heard all over the goldfields.

The most successful songwriter was a miner called John A. Stone, known as Old Put. By chance, he did well out of gold after several average years, and retired to devise new songs to be sung by his troupe that toured the mining camps. His paperback booklet, *The Original California Songster,* sold very well, since the songs were popular.

Many gold-rush songs and mining-camp lyrics were set to tunes such as "Pop Goes the Weasel." The songs told of the trip to California and the arrival in San Francisco. Some dealt with the long sea voyage around Cape Horn, or the trip via Panama. Others told of crossing the plains, a journey that usually had to wait until spring, so that the pack animals could feed on the forage. Yet the wagons had to get through the Sierra passes before the snow had fallen.

Songs about this trip, the best for argonauts from the Midwest, often spoke of Pike—Pike County, Missouri—and of having diarrhea and other troubles en route to Eldorado. Animals as well as men found life difficult. Many never made it.

"Seeing the Elephant," or having one's fill of life, told of going to search for gold. Many songs were of the hard life in the diggings, and among the miners, in the camp and by the campfire. Some told of life in California, of the Chinese, of thieves, and of bank robbers.

Often enough, the miner's lot was not a happy one. Many

"Seeing the Elephant" became a popular expression with the forty-niners. It means seeing all there is to see—and then some. *Courtesy Wells Fargo Bank History Room, San Francisco.*

songs were laments over his fate and troubles. Others told of the homeward trail as the miners packed up and left.

Often enough, mining songs are parodies, or caricatures, ridiculing the mining life. The hard work, sadness, and loneliness of the gold miner in the wilds are found in many of the songs. Yet the gold-rush songs are not songs to work by.

Visitors to the diggings often remarked on the silence of the miners. The thirst for gold, and the labor of acquisition, overruled all else. The mining often totally absorbed all the faculties. Often, complete silence reigned among the miners. They not only addressed not a word to each other, but seemed averse to all conversation.

Some songs may have sounded like sea shanties. Others may have had the sea shanty touch. They may have been sung boisterously. But most were not happy songs. They told of the weather in New York City, of cooking on the overland route, of trouble with Indians, of life on board ship, of buying revolvers, and of searching for the golden fleece.

Most of the gold-rush songs died a natural death fairly quickly after the rush was over. Some lingered on, and the subject itself generated popular songs and general public interest for decades. But few of the songs became part of the musical scene.

Perhaps the great number written compelled the loss of most. They were popular at the time, sung in the saloons and as professional entertainment. Many derived from already popular tunes and adapted old lyrics. Most were written by professional songwriters. Picking a banjo and singing a song in town, or in the pine-clothed hills, was common enough, but most of the songs lasted just a year or two, a few at most.

Somehow, they never linked up with any similar event or earlier historical occasion. That's because the gold rush was new in history. Unlike the plantation songs that drew on generations of a certain type of life, the songs of the gold rush were of high hopes, troubles, and disappointments.

In one sense, the songs of the gold rush parody the whole business of trying to get rich quickly. Some men succeed. So do some nations. Often, men gain by luck or at the expense of others. Only a few have made fortunes out of gold.

The forty-niners never had much of a chance for a fortune, since so many went to pick one up. Perhaps the very business of looking for a fortune in a river, or digging a hole in a hill, excites ridicule even among the participants. Hard songs came from a hard life.

Thus the songs of the gold rush speak eloquently of the gold rush and of much that encircled the life of a forty-niner. But the chancey business of finding a fortune under a rock, in reality a hard grind that broke many miners, is perhaps not a subject to be sung about with glee.

Nor is the type of work suitable for a work song. The optimism and enthusiasm of the raw recruit often soon gave way to despair, as hard toil and meager rewards over the long run spelled the end of the Eldorado dream. A fortune awaited but few. So the miners ridiculed their high hopes in songs, spoke of their experiences en route, in California, of the folks back home, and of leaving the diggings.

The forty-niners were off to California with a banjo on their knee. They found that the gleams of gold were easily missed, that looking at mud and gravel was nothing to be happy about, that eating pork and beans could become monotonous and lead to scurvy.

Stephen Foster's "Oh! Susanna" was the most popular melody, and was sung all over the world. But the usual words sung to it spoke of the high hopes of getting to San Francisco, or California, not of what happened in the diggings. Often enough, of course, it was sung by people who had no intention of going to California. It became a boating song on the Chagres River on the way to Panama. It was sung on the South Atlantic and the Pacific, and by the campfires on the plains.

Other songs came from Tin Pan Alley, the four most notable being "The Gold Digger's Waltz," "The Golden Drag Waltz," "The San Francisco Waltz," and "The Sacramento Gallop." They were popular among those staying at home.

The port of San Francisco was the destination of gold seekers. Here is a rendering of the port in 1849, from a drawing by George H. Baker for the New York *Tribune*. *Courtesy Title Insurance and Trust Company (Los Angeles) Collection of Historical Photographs.*

WHAT THE FORTY-NINERS LEFT, AND WHAT THEY FOUND

When the forty-niners arrived in the land of gold they discovered bustling and busy cities full of young men from all nations preparing for the trip to the mountains. The majority of the gold seekers were native-born Americans. Among foreigners, the largest number came from the British Isles, including Ireland. The free trade policies of Britain had hurt Ireland's agriculture. Labor-saving devices had cut farming employment. The potato famine had forced hundreds of thousands of Irish to emigrate.

From Germany came many young men wishing to avoid Prussian militarism. France and Italy, in the grip of intense political and social change, contributed thousands. Few Russians left for California, but Norway and Sweden saw some of their young men go, even though economic conditions were not harsh. Adventure and the desire to improve their social position provided the impetus. Few Swiss rushed to California.

China, a nation that had been opened up to Western trade and influence only a short time earlier, was suffering from so many problems, including a population explosion, famine, and economic setbacks, that thousands of its subjects flocked to California when the few early Chinese settlers reported success not only in the goldfields but also in business and trade. Chinese miners, preparing their own grub at the diggings, soon discovered that Americans liked the taste of it and were willing to pay in gold! Not too surprisingly, the Chinese restaurant business quickly flourished.

Japan, however, was still a closed world. Even so, a few Japanese turned up to try their luck in the diggings. From Australia came some aborigines, former convicts, and the usual type of gold seeker. New Zealand provided some native Maoris and British settlers. Canada, Mexico, Chile, Peru, and the Pacific islands sent many men, some of them arriving well before the forty-niners from other lands.

Gold itself was the main attraction, of course, but the push in many cases came from economic conditions faced by the emigrants at home. Wages generally were low, although higher in the United States than elsewhere. In 1849, wages in the United States for skilled workers ranged from 90¢ to $2.70 a day. In Massachusetts, for instance, a mechanic got $8 weekly, a laborer $4.50, while the range for industrial workers was from $5 to $10 weekly. In the United States in 1849, a weekly wage of $10 was very good. A farm laborer got $4.

Wages in Europe in 1849 were much lower than in the United States. A bricklayer in France got about 45¢ a day. A farm laborer in Britain received $2.50 weekly. An industrial worker earning over $6 weekly in Europe was well off. Textile workers were usually badly paid. Silk-factory wages ranged from 14¢ to 52¢ daily. In Britain's cotton industry, a spinner got about $1.20 for sixty hours' work. The foreman, called an overlooker, received $7 weekly.

Farm laborers also earned little. In France and Germany, the usual rate was less than $3 weekly. In Britain, a shepherd was paid $125 annually.

Many gold seekers obviously left very little back home, in

monetary terms. The call of gold was irresistible. By and large, they acted according to their financial and social status. A few professional men went to the diggings, including doctors, lawyers, and clergymen. So did businessmen, and the sons of well-to-do families not yet settled in a vocation.

Not all those going to California were gold crazy. Some were out for a good time. Others were land speculators, gamblers, small businessmen, and traders. Just how many emigrants from each nation arrived in California during the gold rush will never be known, since precise accounts never were possible.

But they certainly found a different world. Wages seemed fantastically high. Laboring men in stores earned $125 a month. Boys who cleaned boots and knives received $60. A woman servant, Indian or Chilean, was paid from $40 to $60 monthly. The sums seem small now, but for those days they were generous indeed.

Yet they bought little, for prices were fantastically high also. They were bad enough in San Francisco; in mining communities they were worse. The cost of provisions, clothing, and all the necessities of life was often exorbitant.

Prices, of course, varied from district to district and from time to time. Letters back home and diaries record many harrowing stories. One forty-niner worked eleven days at a digging, made $104 a day, then was taken sick with fever. A doctor from sixty miles away paid four visits, charging $600 altogether, or $150 a visit. That left the miner with $60 in his pocket after he had paid for his provisions.

Others found that $150 in the camps bought less than $30 in New York. Vegetables were scarce. Potatoes were $1 per pound, and cabbages $1 each. The country was difficult to live in. Distances were hard to cover. Prices were high accordingly.

Miners who worked for others often were paid an ounce of gold for a day's work. That gold was worth from $16 to $18 if bought honestly—which was not always the case. In 1848, for instance, so much gold was found by the early gold seekers, including Indians, that the price of gold fell sharply, since the advantage was to the buyer. Many unlucky miners found themselves having to accept almost anything they could get for what they considered their fortune. One gold buyer in the camps picked up thirty-six pounds at $3 an ounce, even though the price back in Monterey was $16 an ounce. American Indians finding gold got as little as 50¢ an ounce late in 1848. White miners sometimes received as little as $1.

After 1848, the price received for gold rose to $10 an ounce, and later ranged from $16 to $18 an ounce. Gold was worth $18 an ounce at the United States Mint in Philadelphia, but much or most of the gold that was found at the diggings contained other metals, such as silver, up to about 10 percent. That brought the local price down to around $17 an ounce. Sometimes, $18 an ounce or more would be paid for gold dust, but some cheating took place in the weighing. Miners often complained of being given a poor price, a low weight, even of buyers who blew away some of the gold dust.

The gold seekers soon discovered that mining gold was a business, with all the tricks of the trade. For an outfit, they needed pick, pan, shovel, blanket, shirts, frying pan, a supply of bacon, flour, and salt, and many other items. Tea and sugar were luxuries.

Forty-niners often found themselves in rough company, associating with disbanded soldiers, gamblers, runaway sailors, and people from all walks of life, all nationalities. Life was tough. Graves of young men of eighteen, nineteen, and twenty already dotted the mining camps.

Some gold seekers preferred working by themselves. That meant using a pan, a type of circular flattish dish. Water was needed, since the basic principle of gold mining was to use the heavy weight of gold to concentrate it in payable form. Gravel or dirt was put in the pan, water added, and the pan swirled. Since gold was about seven or eight times heavier than the soil or gravel, the water would rinse the dirt over the pan, leaving the gold at the bottom.

Often, of course, no gold was seen. Gold was called color. "Not even the color" meant that no gold had been seen in the pan. Gold stood out, of course, against the dark mud and soil and the white of the crushed quartz.

Many miners soon learned that panning for gold was hard work, yielding few rewards. By forming partnerships and working with larger equipment, miners could process more gravel, rock, or silt per man.

One popular device was the cradle, or rocker, similar to a child's cradle. The principle, of course, was the same as with the pan, in that the gold sank while the water washed the rock away. The use of mercury, or quicksilver, to recover gold, especially the fine gold dust or powder that could easily be carried away, was also common. Mercury could safely be put in the bottom of the pan, rocker, or even larger equipment. The gold was "wetted" by the mercury and became brittle, losing its color. This amalgam, being heavier than mercury, sank, and was recovered. Heating the amalgam then drove off the mercury, leaving the gold. The process sometimes caused eye damage.

The tom, or long tom, was basically a trough fitted with riffles, as was the cradle, to help catch the gold. Later, sluice boxes, often strings of them, were used as a form of extended long tom.

This way of separating the gold from the mud and crushed rock with water took place in wet diggings. Dry diggings had little or no water, so water had to be brought in by diverting a stream or building an aqueduct, usually of wood. All sorts of contraptions were devised to bring the water to the payable gold digging. Otherwise, the gold had to be separated from powdered dried mud by winnowing, as in separating wheat from chaff. Often, even the gold dust was blown away too, so great effort and expense went into bringing water to the diggings. Otherwise, the dry diggings could not operate on a mass-production basis, and the yields usually were small.

od of Auburn ravine
California
the early 50's

As gold became more difficult to find, in the early 1850s miners from many nations formed teams and used a variety of equipment. *Courtesy Wells Fargo Bank History Room, San Francisco.*

Both wet and dry diggings were alluvial or placer mines, having been transported by water at one time or another. The shift of a stream, or the advent of a dry season, would turn a wet placer into a dry one, but both were alluvial deposits, in contrast to lode mines, which consisted of quartz gold-bearing veins in rock. Gold miners soon realized that digging out the rock and crushing it was the same as nature's way of breaking up the rock by water erosion and transporting the debris down the stream. As the pickings from the alluvial deposits grew slim, miners started digging into hard rock. The work was getting tougher all the time.

More and more capital was needed also. Even a rocker or cradle cost from $50 to $100 by early 1849. The more productive long toms and sluices were usually beyond the financial reach of individual miners, and, of course, they had to be worked in partnerships, or by employing miners on a daily basis.

As the months passed, the nature of mining changed from one of relative simplicity to mass-production methods using more and more expensive but crude-looking equipment, built on the spot or nearby. Later still, corporate capitalism moved in, and the really big mining works got under way, employing powerful hoses to break up rocks and huge stamping mills to crush gold-bearing ore.

Hydraulicking, as the use of powerful hoses was called, began around 1852 and continued for three decades until it was stopped because of damage to crops and rivers.

The day of the lonely miner with pick, shovel, and pan was soon over. As thousands poured over the ridges and slopes of the foothills, the pickings per man grew small. By late 1849 and early 1850, letters of complaint were common. Newcomers wrote home that they had no place to try their luck. Much gold was being dug, but thousands were digging it. The expense was great, the labor hard. The gold rush had become a dog's life. Miners became unhappy, lonesome, cured of their roving disposition.

The visions of gold had turned into staring at mud. A panning that yielded 25¢ in gold was now rich, even though from $1 to $5 per pan was sometimes found. A fair prospect was a bit, or 12½¢ to the pan. Many miners could pan fifty or sixty times in a day for a return of $10 or so. That return was handsome compared with wages back east, in Europe, or in China, but it was usually spent at the diggings where prices were exorbitant.

Using a rocker could produce much more gold per person in the partnership. Even so, the great days of 1848 and 1849 were over. By August 1850, only one in a hundred was making a decent wage in the goldfields. Only one in a thousand actually was rewarded for all the trouble he had taken getting to California. By then, of course, the big winners were those who stole—the gamblers, the traders, and the tavern keepers. A week of hardship, toil, and exposure, rocking sixty buckets a day for six days, would bring in some seven or eight ounces of gold, worth about $140. Yet it bought goods that would have cost only $25 or less in New York. The effort was no longer worth it.

The good old days when a lucky miner could find a fortune in the bed of a stream had changed to panning that yielded "not even the color."

As disappointment and frustration set in, violence grew and the ugliness of failure developed. The blistered hands and bleeding fingers of back-breaking work generated a hatred of the successful, of the foreigners with nonwhite faces, strange speech, and unusual clothes, of those who charged the high prices.

Indeed, some forty-niners had made their presence felt from the very beginning. The American Indians, who for generations had roamed the mountains and valleys, really suffered. Partly that was due to California's coming under the United States after the Mexican War. But Indians were also driven off their lands by gold seekers, herded into reservations, killed off either by shooting or by infectious diseases, or harmed by postwar military measures taken on the grounds of security.

The many native-born Californios, those of Spanish-Mexican descent, were not affected very much at first, since the gold had been discovered in the north and many of the Californios lived in the south. They gained from higher prices for their meat, but later they suffered the loss of their estates as the gold seekers and other migrants swarmed over the south as well as the north.

Others who regarded the gold discovery as a calamity were those who had received huge land grants from Mexico. Among these, ironically, was the Cap'n, or Old Cap, John Augustus Sutter, the man on whose property the 1848 gold discovery had been made. His land was grabbed, and he spent a fortune in legal fees trying to get it back. Another marked for misfortune was his millwright, James Marshall, who had found the gold in the tailrace of the sawmill he was building for Sutter. The influx of miners, and disputes with them, forced Marshall to leave his own mining claims and roam the ravines looking for new gold deposits.

Gold was clearly a misfortune for many already settled in California in 1848. How did the forty-niners fare? The history of the California gold rush is virtually told in the curious names of some of the mining camps and diggings: Bed Bug, You Bet, Whisky Slide, Poverty Flat, Loafer Hill, Grub Gulch, Poker Flat, Gouge Eye, Slapjack Bar, Strawberry Valley, Port Wine, Sweet Revenge, Grass Valley, Greenhorn Creek, Carson Hill, Git-up-and-Git, Black Gulch Camp, Murderer's Bar, Railroad Flat, Mad Mule Gulch, Pleasant Valley, Red Dog Camp, Fiddletown, Drytown, and Rough and Ready.

Rough and ready indeed the mining communities were. Although some solitary miners preferred to rough it in the wilds, many sought the company of other goldbugs in camps, the tent towns to which the miners returned at night.

Several such camps, but sometimes just one, formed a mining district that included specific gulches, ran to the top of certain divides, took in named flats and ridges, and, within these limits, expanded as new gold discoveries were made and new camps sprang into being, often almost overnight.

Dissatisfied miners would sometimes form a new mining district from an existing large one if they felt so inclined and if they could persuade other fellow miners to secede. Usually they were impatient with the local mining claim regulations, feeling that different conditions in a mining area far removed from the original camp justified a change in control—to themselves, of course.

If settled conditions prevailed for any length of time, camps grew into towns of wooden structures. Over the years, places altered their names as conditions changed, or were abandoned and left to rot when the gold ran out. Thus Dry Diggings became Hangtown, and then, with the arrival of respectability, Placerville. By and large, the camp sites and diggings were not given happy names. Little joy can be found in words such as "bug," "bet," "whisky," "poverty," "grub," "poker," "gouge," "slapjack," "greenhorn," "murderer," "rough," or "hang."

The impression is of a hard life with many difficulties, a life of violence, gambling, drinking, and taking advantage of others. Yet there must have been excitement along with the tragedies.

Most of the gold seekers were men, young or in their early middle age. Few of them knew much about gold, although some had worked gold in Georgia, North Carolina, New Mexico, and Mexico. The others had to, and did, learn fast. Some of the forty-niners were tough pioneers or their adventurous sons on their way westward.

A few from other lands were skilled miners, including gold seekers from Chile, Peru, Germany, Wales, and a small number from Russia. But most of the forty-niners were neither miners nor pioneers. They learned the hard way in the mountains and ravines of the Sierra. They aged rapidly as they worked in the icy mountain streams, panning for gold, sometimes in the hot sun, at other times in canyons that always seemed cold and sunless.

Finding gold, they discovered, was hard work, often disappointing. The golden magnet had pulled them thousands of miles, but before too long they usually discovered that Eldorado, the gilded, had a face of gold but a heart of rock. Many of them had left hard work and low wages for the chance of picking up a fortune. Some ended up with even harder work than the job back home and lower wages, in terms of buying power.

That was bad enough. Worse was the violence that came when former convicts, gamblers, thieves, cheats, and murderers mixed with the honest citizenry and genuine gold seekers.

San Francisco, the major port of entry to the gold mines, was soon the scene of social unrest and a crime wave. The violence spread not only to the mining communities that were scattered far and wide over the Sierra but to the settlements and cattle ranches of the south, far, far away from the thought of gold.

In San Francisco itself, the point was reached when an outraged public decided to do something about it. In short, the citizenry took the law into their own hands. Who else was there to enforce some semblance of civilized living, not only in San Francisco but in the other cities of the coast, the mining camps, the cattle ranches tucked away in valleys, and the small settlements that for years had slept peacefully in the sunshine?

LEAVE TOWN—OR ELSE!

The first roughnecks arrived in San Francisco in 1848, and the gold rush quickly generated conflicting stories of romance and violence, law-abiding citizens and murderers, hardship and boisterousness, justice and lynchings. All of them were true, and not surprisingly, since an established way of life that had been changing only very slowly over the decades suddenly erupted into a new type of society.

The early forty-eighters, as we have seen, were already living in California at the time of the gold discovery. They went looking for gold out of fun, excitement, and, no doubt, a natural desire to get something for very little effort. Many had been born in California. Others were there for furs, farming, trading, or shipping.

These early gold seekers, then, were simply local citizens who believed in law and order. Little theft occurred in the summer of 1848, and very few disorders. Matters such as the size of claim to be allowed were discussed by the miners in camp meetings.

These small early mining camps gradually expanded into mining districts dominated by honesty and hospitality. Disputes arose, of course, but they normally were settled in friendly fashion and by majority vote, since all involved were Californians who already had a job, a home, and a stake in the community. Looking for gold was simply an unexpected fringe benefit.

Life changed alarmingly when the first ruffians and roughnecks began visiting the otherwise peaceful foothills, mining camps, and valleys. These thugs were interested not in working for gold, but in stealing it or cheating for it. They were reinforced in 1849 by many more—along with tens of thousands of genuine goldbugs.

By the summer of 1849, the peace, orderly behavior, and hard work of the early camps had given way to theft and murder, which soon became common not only in the cities along the coast, but in the outlying mining areas and the smaller settlements scattered here and there in the foothills and valleys.

The structure of the mining camps also changed as the months and years passed. Conditions varied from camp to camp. The first white tents were pitched beside the rivers and beneath the tall pines. Rude cabins rose rapidly. Soon a group of tents, cabins, flimsy board shanties, and combinations of canvas, brush, and stones in the shade of a tree, formed a camp. The growth, of course, was disorderly. Mining claims soon conflicted. Disputes arose.

Before long, more substantial structures had been built in the more profitable mining camps. The miners were followed by merchants and whisky peddlers, gamblers and gold buyers. Those skilled in trades, crafts, and professions also made their appearance. Soon saloons, general stores, restaurants, blacksmith shops, newspaper offices, gold assay stores, and express offices became the center of a much larger community to which the diggers returned whenever possible. Later came the stage depot, the firehouse, the church, the cemetery, and various places of entertainment.

Even by the end of 1848, mining or prospecting had begun

along some two hundred miles of the Sierra Nevada. The unusual gold quartz deposits worked by the miners in one form or another, placer or lode, were concentrated in an area known as the Mother Lode that ran for some seventy miles between Mariposa and Amador.

The mines became known as northerly and southerly, divided by the watershed between the Cosumnes and Mokelumne rivers. The northerly diggings were mainly in a compact district on the American and Feather rivers and their tributaries. The southern mines stretched down to the Merced River and the mountains and valleys of the San Joaquin River.

Since the miners roamed far and wide, no sharp distinctions can easily be made between the northern and southern mines. Even in the early days, however, the northern mines tended to have log cabins and frame houses, while those in the south had tents and canvas. The northern mines tended to be worked by Americans, while Mexicans and Latin Americans were more often found in the south.

As more and more miners arrived, greater amounts of gold were produced. The solitary miner with his simple pan was supplemented now by partnerships, even companies, using equipment that had to be stopped and cleaned for its gold every so often. This meant that much gold, often in the form of the amalgam with mercury, even nuggets, was left in the machine overnight, making stealing a worthwhile occupation for the unscrupulous. Whereas in 1848, gold often had been left lying around, now it had to be protected. Buckskin and doeskin bags were universally used for this purpose.

The unofficial courts set up by the miners, or by local vigilantes that kept order in their mining camp or district, usually meted out justice on Sundays. Special cases, such as the hated thieving of gold, were sometimes dealt with immediately on the spot—and ruthlessly. A thief, if found, was lucky to escape with a whipping. Some were sent packing. Violent crimes such as murder were punished by hanging, or lynching.

Similar goings-on occurred in San Francisco and the other rapidly growing cities of the coast and inland plains. Until the California gold rush, new settlements had grown slowly over the years. By and large, although a system of justice was not easily maintained, it developed in line with the gradual growth of the city or settlement.

San Francisco grew so greatly in population so quickly from gold that justice was very hard to administer. By early 1849, clippers, steamers, and other vessels were bringing thousands of newcomers, and the hard-working citizens of San Francisco were discovering that gold and gold seekers meant trouble.

The first serious trouble for San Francisco arose not from foreigners arriving from outside the United States, but from displaced New Yorkers and others from the East. Mainly a regiment of New York volunteers fresh home from the Mexican War, they called themselves the Hounds, and operated from a canvas structure on Kearny Street known as Tammany Hall, in honor of the political establishment in New York's Manhattan.

Since San Francisco then had no police force, the Hounds were completely free to make public nuisances of themselves. They would go into stores and walk out without paying, or enjoy a meal in a restaurant, start acting rowdy, and again leave without paying, or get thrown out.

By the standards of the following years in San Francisco, the Hounds were petty criminals. But the good citizens of San Francisco had grown fearful of what was happening. A major fire on May 4, 1849, quickly produced a committee of safety. When the Hounds attacked the quarters occupied by immigrants from Chile in July 1849, a police force of 230 was formed, and the Hounds found themselves hounded. That was the last of the Hounds. They escaped serious punishment, since justice was difficult to enforce and escaping was easy enough.

A far more serious threat to the good life in San Francisco arose from some Australian immigrants. The British had established a penal colony in Australia to which they sent convicts. Many of these men had been deported from Britain for relatively trivial or political crimes, but some were hardened convicts. In 1850, many of them came to San Francisco.

They lived mostly in Sydneytown, a city within a city, sprawling near the base of Telegraph Hill, a slum of tents, small hovels, disreputable rooming houses, dubious gambling joints, and cheap groggeries. These Australian immigrants became known as Sydney Coves, Sydney Birds, or Sydney Ducks. The name that stuck was Sydney Ducks.

The term "duck" came from Tasmania, the largest Australian penal settlement, known in those days as Van Dieman's Land. Released prisoners would go by boat up the River Derwent to Hobart, often accompanied by thousands of wildfowl. These ex-convicts became known in Australia as Derwenters, and in San Francisco as Ducks.

Even by the summer of 1849, earlier Australian immigrants had made themselves so obnoxious in San Francisco that vessels from Australia were inspected, doubtful characters were prevented from landing, and those already in the city were advised to leave.

The Sydney Ducks had a frightening method of operating. They would decoy someone to the edge of a cliff, rob or kill him, then push the body over the edge. The Ducks operated in gang fashion.

Other criminals, of course, were to be found in San Francisco, but the Ducks were the main target of an outraged public fearful of robbery, alarmed by arson, and wondering what was coming next.

In June 1851 the citizens organized to suppress the desperadoes, including the Sydney Ducks. The Ducks and others were hunted, ruthless measures were adopted, and the Ducks were no more. Several were executed, and many more banished, mostly back to Sydney. After operating for three months that summer and dealing with many suspected criminals, the vigilantes disbanded in September.

Some mining communities became infamous for their law-enforcement activities. Hangtown was famous for its "hanging tree" (at the left of the building marked Empire). *Courtesy Title Insurance and Trust Company (Los Angeles) Collection of Historical Photographs.*

But worse was to come. By 1856, the city government was so corrupt, justice so difficult to obtain, and crime so rampant that the San Francisco vigilantes rose again. This time, they held paramilitary parades and frightened the wits out of other law-abiding citizens, who began to feel that the cure offered by the vigilantes was worse than the disease caused by thugs and murderers. The public became worried. Politics took over the problem when the vigilantes were opposed by the Law and Order party. An election was held.

Fortunately, the vigilantes had the good sense to realize they had grown too big for their britches and were becoming hated themselves. They disbanded without too much fuss, working in the future as citizens through the usual political processes.

In addition to the vigilantes of San Francisco, the mining communities and other cities also had their own vigilantes, some far less respectful of others' rights than were those in the city.

One mining camp quickly got the name of Hangtown from the miners' willingness to enforce their laws by stringing from a nearby tree those summarily convicted. The hanging tree remained famous, even after Hangtown, earlier known as Dry Diggings, discreetly changed its name to Placerville when violence subsided. Public hangings were not uncommon during the California gold rush, so an undue emphasis should not be placed on Hangtown, San Francisco, or particular groups of thugs.

Crime simply had gotten out of hand. So did vigilantism, especially when it was organized into paramilitary parades, with certificates of membership, badges of organized committees of vigilance, and a formal organization that simply did not have the approval of the citizens. The vigilantes took on some of the frightening characteristics of a police state.

Yet the committees of vigilantes grew out of a desperate need. They were similar in many respects to the committees of miners that governed the mining communities in the gold-mining areas. Even these groups were capable of gross abuses, as we have seen in Hangtown, but normally they operated on majority vote and the consent of the governed. The vigilantes, as they finally were seen by the public, were self-appointed to an organization that had no true public support. They were not a local government elected by the people but a separate clique with many of the trappings of a summary police force outside the law.

The citizens of San Francisco finally sensed the basic nature of this frightening paramilitary rigmarole. And when they did, they got rid of it, bag and baggage.

10

WE DON'T LIKE YOUR LOOKS!

The vigilantism of California's early years is now no more. It was supplanted by normal judicial processes arising out of elected local governments. But the discrimination on grounds of race, color, and national origin that became such a feature of the gold rush years was—and is—more persistent.

We must not, of course, be harsh on California, since most of the gold bugs had been born elsewhere and were simply using California as a place to get rich quick. When the going got tough, the tough got ruthless. By and large, the discrimination was not unique to the West, even though it had the unusual trappings of gold and the influx of many immigrants from China.

The story of gold rush discrimination is the old tale of man's inhumanity to man. The colonists who first settled these United States over three centuries ago came out of a desire to escape one form or another of oppression—and to improve their lot in life. They themselves hated the discrimination and injustices they had to face in the countries they came from, yet they did not hesitate to enforce their own strongly held religious and other views when differences of opinion arose in their new country. Nor did they shrink from killing off the Indians, taking their land, and importing blacks from Africa to do the dirty work at low pay and often under horrible conditions. The ends justified the means, they seemed to feel. The same was true in California.

Until 1848, California had been developing very slowly. The years following 1840 had seen a marked interest in American involvement in the Pacific coastal area, but the very difficulty of getting to California and the Oregon country from the East precluded any major American colonization in the absence of very special circumstances, such as the gold rush provided.

For centuries, American Indians had hunted and gathered food in the hills, valleys, and plains of California. No doubt the Spanish settlers and missions had used the Indians for their own benefit, but by and large the Indians had been treated as human beings, even protected and helped by the Spanish missions.

Changes occurred when Mexico took over—that is, when it declared its independence of Spain. Yet Californian life continued to be very open and leisurely. One reason, of course, was the small population in a large territory. Mexico took no great interest in developing its northerly territory. The emphasis was on cattle. Some mining was undertaken. The rich deposits of quicksilver in the form of cinnabar had received some attention in Mexico City. Otherwise, life continued very much the same as under Spain—with certain exceptions.

The decline of the Spanish missions meant that American Indians had to fend for themselves or work on Mexican ranches. The gold rush made drastic changes inevitable, both for American Indians and the Mexicans and Spanish-Mexicans living in California.

Assessing just what would have happened without the gold rush is not easy, since changes would have taken place with the conquest of California by the United States. That the gold rush should have happened almost simultaneously with

American acquisition of California is a major historical coincidence, but it confuses a clear judgment on the impact of the gold rush.

Certainly, life became very difficult for many of those already living in California in the war period, 1846–1848. The arrival of the new or postwar American settlers meant that American Indians now faced people who were often hostile. The early American settlers in California were few in number and had gotten along fairly well with the Indians. The acquisition of California by the United States placed the official seal on the new state of affairs. The gold rush put the new views quickly into practice. Thousands of Indians died of starvation or from disease in the next two decades. Indians often were hunted by the new settlers. Their lands were stolen. The rush of gold-seeking immigrants was a disaster for the Indians.

Mexicans, too, found themselves the object of race wars. The Californios of Spanish-Mexican descent also were in the way of the newcomers who wanted land for one reason or another. In short, it was out with the old and in with the new. The newly arrived Americans, including gold seekers, wanted what the others had. By and large, they took it.

The forty-niners and many of the miners who came later were a rough lot, living a tough life under difficult conditions. As more miners came and gold mining became increasingly precarious, discrimination and injustice in the mines became common. It spread among the general population as newcomers arrived from all over the world. Those who were non-white, or spoke a language other than English, often found themselves the object of gross discrimination.

That this attitude developed is understandable. Foreigners were picking up gold, while many Americans were finding life tough!

Mexicans were at a particular disadvantage, since they had lost the war. However, Mexicans who had already worked placer gold deposits in Mexico or in New Mexico naturally wished to try their hand in the new diggings. Often they taught newcomers how to pan and look for gold. As the better deposits were worked out and the toil became harder, the Mexicans often were pushed aside, even forced to leave and go back south.

Other forty-niners who found themselves in trouble with the dominant Americans were those from Chile. They had received early news of the gold find from ships on their way from San Francisco to New York in the summer of 1848. Many Chileans arrived in the goldfields before other forty-niners had even set off. Partly because so many ships rounding the Horn called at Valparaiso in Chile, and partly because Chile was then the major trading nation on the entire Pacific coast, north and south of the Equator, South Americans were generally referred to as Chileans, even though other nationalities, such as Peruvians, were included.

Gold seekers from France also found themselves lumped in with the Chileans. The French miners tended to be clannish and to mix mainly with the South Americans. The French were known as Keskydees, after the French question *Qu'est-ce qu'il dit?* (What is he saying?).

Chinese, usually not a migratory people, were seldom seen in California before 1848, but conditions in China forced many to leave and settle all over the Pacific in the search for a better life. The Californian goldfields and the opportunity for business in San Francisco soon attracted Chinese by the thousands. Fears that the teeming millions of China would soon be settling in California helped generate widespread discrimination against Chinese immigrants in the cities and in the goldfields. Chinese miners tended to protect themselves by working hard in the poorer gold deposits, but their frugality, coupled with their usually having some money on hand, aroused resentment among other miners, especially Americans. Yet the Chinese had originally been welcome in California. Most preferred to stay in cosmopolitan centers such as San Francisco than risk their lives and fortunes in the diggings.

By late 1849 and early 1850, the increasingly tough conditions in the diggings and the arrival of more and more gold seekers, often from foreign lands, made life extremely difficult for many Mexicans, Chinese, Chileans, and Indians. Some foreigners, such as those from Britain, were usually treated fairly and included with native Americans when it came to discriminating against foreigners. The German immigrant, despite language problems, also felt little discrimination.

Yet the pressures to do something about foreign miners mounted, especially as the pickings grew slimmer. Guards were hired to watch the claims, thefts of gold were common in the camps and even from the gold-mining machinery and equipment, and more and more miners became desperate. Strong-arm tactics in the mines already had forced many foreign miners out, but something more was needed, they felt.

Politicians responded to the pressure. The Foreign Miners' License Law of 1850 was enacted to discourage mining by non-Americans. The $20 monthly tax imposed by this law on immigrant miners forced many to leave the diggings penniless and return home.

The tax was used against the Chinese, Spanish-Americans, and French with great effectiveness. Some, of course, were unwilling to submit to tax discrimination and refused to pay and defended themselves. Other miners abandoned their claim, a clear indication that it was not then worth the effort, even if only $20, just over an ounce of gold, had to be paid. The days of fortunes for the picking clearly were over. Others took up jobs in the cities.

So great was the exodus from the mines that shopkeepers and traders started complaining. Prices fell, and local business recessions began. The tax was repealed in 1851, and revised and reenacted in 1852 at $3 monthly. This new tax yielded more than the original $20 tax, an indication that the earlier rate had been levied deliberately to force out many foreign miners.

Strong-arm action continued in the mines, making life generally difficult for those with a different appearance or speaking another tongue. Those who were English or blond usually got along well with native Americans. Included in the favored group were Irish, Scandinavian, German, and British immigrants. Others, such as the French, Spanish-Americans, and American blacks, often found life miserable. Australians, probably because their numbers included former convicts, also were included among those compelled to leave the diggings, even leave California.

Assessing racial and other forms of discrimination is never simple, since it comes in so many forms and in so many degrees. Many Chinese, for instance, continued to work in the mines, as well as in San Francisco. That applied also to gold seekers from South America and Mexico. American Indians worked alongside whites in the diggings. So did American blacks. Some were slaves or former slaves. A few made enough to buy their freedom. They worked hard, digging out the gravel or rock and putting it through the various types of gold-washing equipment. Generally, however, blacks were unwelcome and unwanted. Fugitive slaves often found themselves badly treated. Even though California was nonslaveholding territory, strong Southern sympathies abounded, in sharp contrast with those in Northern states.

The discrimination of the early mining days made an unpleasant mark on the life of California. Orientals especially suffered greatly at the hands of a predominant white society. That fact is seen in the history of discriminatory legislation and in the political, social, and economic injustice that seriously harmed the fabric of Californian society long after gold had ceased to be so important.

Discrimination, of course, is often rooted in economic self-interest, which gives it a particular viciousness because so much—standard of living, social prestige, even life itself—often is at stake. Fear of strange ways, different cultures, unusual languages, dress, and customs combines with racial and color prejudice to produce social attitudes that flourish for decades, remaining an evil, albeit sometimes hidden, prejudice that can easily be aroused should any new threat appear.

The gold rush in California gave the state a very bad start in race relations. Of course, slavery was then legal in the United States—an indication of the general public attitude. Also, a nation with a population as immense as China's could easily send hundreds of thousands to California, turning it almost into a Chinese province. Other nations have faced similar problems and have responded similarly.

These mitigating factors have to be considered when we view the impact of the gold rush on the treatment of non-white minorities in California. Even so, the record from gold-rush days on is bad. Fortunately, recent decades have seen much improvement. The excesses of history are, we can now hope, things of the past. Yet the forced resettlement of California's Japanese-Americans during World War II is a painful reminder that old prejudices, like old fires, easily come to life with a little blowing.

One fact to note is that the foreign-born population of California continued to rise after the gold rush. Obviously, many foreigners, if not most, found themselves well treated. In 1850, foreigners made up only a quarter of California's population. By 1860, nearly two-fifths were foreign born. By then, gold was no longer a major attraction, but the spell of the Golden West had achieved a permanent place in world history.

11

THE RIPPLES FROM THE RUSH

The ripples of the California gold rush spread far and wide. It was the first of its kind for three reasons. First, gold naturally is scarce. Few countries have much of it. Second, the gold in most countries had been exploited for the benefit of local or colonial rulers. California gold was wide open to all newcomers. Third, earlier discoveries had been made when getting to the site was almost impossible, except as part of an authorized expedition financed by royalty or the wealthy.

California obviously had gold in abundance. Most of the land was up for grabs, and was not controlled either locally or from afar, even though some large Mexican land grants had been made. Prospectors could get there, some fairly quickly, some after months of hardship, but at least they could get to California within a reasonable time. This combination made the California gold rush a completely unexpected phenomenon. No one had ever thought that sleepy Spanish-Mexican California with its hide and tallow trade would be transformed almost overnight into the site of a worldwide gold mania. It took time for the golden news to sink in. When it did, the rush was truly on.

It was followed by similar gold rushes, to Australia in 1851, Colorado in 1858, South Africa in 1886, and the Klondike in 1898. Nevada had a major silver rush, and South Africa also enjoyed a diamond rush. California gold probably had a greater total impact than any of the others except for the gold and diamonds of South Africa. Those discoveries, which were of monumental importance to South Africa, are worked to this day, several generations after the first finds. The Australian goldfields soon outproduced California's and Australia's population trebled in a decade, but that gain was small compared with California's.

The worldwide emotional impact of the gold rush was profound. Songs were written about it long after the event. Famous writers, such as Mark Twain and Bret Harte, sensed that it belonged in the pages of history as something special. It was just that. Today, especially in the United States with its high standard of living for many and its extensive educational system, we tend to forget that the gold rush happened while Charles Dickens in England was writing of terrible conditions among industrial workers. The right to vote in Europe was limited to a few. Educational opportunities were scarce. Social and political conditions were oppressive in many lands.

The gold rush emphasized man's right to equality and opportunity. It proved that many of the victimized in many lands wished to emigrate to improve their lot. In terms of national emotion, the gold rush was the greatest event between the Declaration of Independence and the Civil War. Internationally, it was as stunning as the Declaration of Independence and the French Revolution. The gold rush exploded on the world scene as a new and startling declaration of independence by the international masses. It was a revolution that insisted on man's right to be equal and live free.

That gold was discovered in California in the same year that revolutions swept Europe is, of course, a coincidence, but the impact was not. The freedom being sought in

Europe, usually unsuccessfully, was the same as the freedom that so many forty-niners hoped for in California. Many did not find it, but for a time at least they enjoyed the exhilaration of sailing the world filled with hope.

The coming of the California gold rush so soon after the largely frustrated revolutions in Europe in 1848 caused great concern among the ruling classes there. While the public generally looked on the discovery of gold with fascination, and wondered whether to join the rush to California, others were not so enthusiastic. Earlier, of course, newspapers and magazines had seldom mentioned distant and undeveloped Mexican California, let alone San Francisco or gold mining.

Great Britain took a particular interest in the phenomenon, partly out of self-interest, since Britain was then the only major nation on the gold standard. By early 1849, Britons were talking excitedly about the new Eldorado. John Bull, as England was called, went crazy about it.

But an attitude of sour grapes and ridicule soon became apparent in some circles. Magazines and newspapers, such as the London *Times* and *The Economist,* provided responsible coverage, usually through New York sources, but the general attitude of the ruling classes is perhaps best seen in the pages of *Punch,* a humorous magazine that often dealt most perceptively with political, economic, and social matters.

Punch declared that the effect of the gold rush would be to raise prices, ruin fools, demoralize a new country first, and settle it afterward—not too bad a description of what happened. *Punch* believed that those who were going to California were people for whom the United States was not big enough and England too hot. Two types would be found in California, *Punch* declared: those who went to clean out the gold and those who went to clean out the gold cleaners.

A newspaper report that a California donkey, laden with gold, had escaped, prompted *Punch* to suggest that other donkeys also had gone wild. If this donkey, said *Punch,* ever

A REGULAR GOLD DUSTMAN.

"Hollo! Where are you off to now?"

"Oh! I ain't a going to stop here, looking for Teaspoons in Cinders. I'm off to Kallifornier, vere there's heaps o' Gold Dust to be had for the Sweepin'."

Britain was agog with the gold rush in 1849. The magazine *Punch* pictured a street sweeper or dustman leaving for California on the fast sailing ship *Moonshine*. *Reproduced by permission of* Punch.

gets out with all that gold, he'll be the cleverest donkey in California.

The magazine suggested that a good outfit to take to California would include a rifle, a pair of good revolvers, a bowie knife, a dirk, and swords. *Punch* also played around with the term "gold dust," since garbage collectors in Britain are known as dustmen. A cartoon showed a regular dustman off to California to sweep up gold dust. Better that, he said, than looking for teaspoons in cinders.

One drawing showed a starving gold miner sitting by his huge pile of gold. In another, the American eagle was suggested as the fastest way to get to California—just climb on board. Still another showed the earth with a lump bitten out, indicating the diggings in the new goldfields. The River Thames was pictured as full of ships, all heading for California.

References were also made to slavery. Of course, discussion was then raging in the United States about the extension of slavery to California. *Punch* declared that many Americans were becoming slaves to gold.

An amusing story in *Punch* told about a laundress who was offering her washing tub for use on a gold-washing expedition to California. The big industrial city of Birmingham, in the English Midlands, it was reported, had received an order for 10,000 shovels, prompting *Punch* to quip that in the game of fortune, spades will be trumps. And the news that a tinware house was selling dustpans for the collection of gold dust brought forth the comment that a lot of dust had already found its way into the eyes of the public in England, as well as in America.

A drawing entitled "A Few Days In The Diggins" showed Yankees in California picking up gold and silver. A similar drawing was headed "The Country For Convicts." In 1849, Australia was objecting to being used as a dumping ground for convicts deported from Britain. Mr. Punch, according to the article, had honored the Home Secretary (the Cabinet

77

Minister responsible for criminals) with an audience. Apparently, the Home Secretary, Sir George Grey, was completely puzzled to know what to do with rogues and thieves. Why not, said Mr. Punch after scratching his head, send the rascals to California?

The gold rush encouraged one writer to produce a one-act play, called *Cockneys in California, or A Piece of Golden Opportunity.* It contained such suggestions as:

> Sell your tables—sell your chairs;
> Sell your mangles—
> Sell your mangles;—
> Sell your feather beds—who cares?
> We'll have spangles—
> We'll have spangles!
>
> Come with shovel, pick, and spade,
> Pan and ladle;—pan and ladle;
> Digging gold's your only trade!
> Bring a cradle;—bring a cradle.
>
> Gold, gold, gold!
> The yellow ore we find;
> In love, in peace, in war,
> 'Tis gold that rules mankind.

Britons obviously found the gold rush of great personal interest or full of acid humor, according to taste. The excitement died away fairly quickly as 1849 passed into 1850. California, almost absent from comment before 1848, mainly because it was not on the world scene and belonged to Mexico, entered public gossip with the gold rush. It became and remained the Land of the Golden West. The golden age, said *Punch,* had come at last.

The French also were keenly interested in the land of golden opportunity. A bevy of French ladies representing the world's oldest profession decided to ply their trade far away from the Left Bank. French government officials, having recently suffered a revolution, discreetly encouraged the emigration of malcontents. Various societies of emigration were formed by interested parties. A lottery was devised by the Société de l'Ingot d'Or, (the Golden Ingot Company), under which some four thousand Frenchmen eventually were shipped to Eldorado. Retired French soldiers officially were helped to go to California. Similar ideas sprouted in other European countries suffering from the threat of revolution.

Yet some countries were not too keen to see their citizens depart for the promised land. Australia and New Zealand, then being settled by the British, needed all the immigrants they could get—except, of course, convicts. These, Australia happily saw depart for California, and wished them well.

While other nations were naturally looking after their own interests at home and in their overseas possessions, the major impact of the gold rush was, of course, felt in California, soon to become a state. California quickly grew into a prosperous community, since it had the three basic necessities for success: a rising population, adequate employment, and sufficient capital. Any prosperous state or nation shows all three. California in those early gold-rush years had an abundance of each.

The wry comment that California was getting rich not because of the gold, but from all the money being sent there to look for gold, is perfectly valid. A vast influx of young men with money, working hard to produce gold, would stimulate even an industrialized economy, even today, let alone a sparsely populated cattle province.

The rush of immigrants, the search for gold, and the flood of capital to mine gold turned California into a busy, bustling, prosperous state that developed many businesses and trading interests based on gold. The rapid growth of San Francisco put Los Angeles at a disadvantage literally for decades, although Los Angeles was the larger in 1849.

The demand for mining supplies, food, and clothing could not immediately be supplied by California. Much had to be imported, often from the East. The shipping activity in the harbors of Boston, New York, Philadelphia, Baltimore, and

New Orleans testified to the business boom created by the gold rush. Shipping goods, as well as forty-niners, to California, brought fortuncs to many.

Merchandise of all kinds was sent to Eldorado. Clothing and flour, those obvious necessities, went in quantity along with calico, cotton goods, broadcloths, wire sieves, hoes, shovels, pickaxes, baskets, and bags. One young man who went was called Levi Strauss. He was soon selling strong pants that quickly became known as Levi's.

Expeditions were organized. Companies were formed. Shipping lines were flooded with inquiries. The outfitting of emigrants became in itself a minor industry, since it included supplies for the overland trip, for the voyage via Chagres in Panama, and for the long haul around Cape Horn.

This business was welcome for many reasons, since trade in general was bad. The end of the Mexican War had cancelled many war contracts. The release of the army from active service had left many unemployed. The ripple effect of the gold rush swept across the world as foreign nations joined the rush to export goods to Eldorado.

The emigration to California, of course, was a form of quick colonization. California, even without gold, would sooner or later have attracted emigrants by the thousand, but the gold discovery meant that at least ten years' migration was squeezed into one year alone—1849. The gold rush as a whole must have given California a boost worth some thirty years of migration. That excludes, of course, the longer-term effects deriving from California's historic association with gold.

In terms of mining, the gold rush meant the start of the system of open or free mining that spread to other states in the West, such as Nevada. In short, miners could make claims and work them if they got there first. In placer, that is, alluvial, deposits swept down by streams, the discoverer owned that particular site. In lode mines, where metal-bearing veins ran through rock, the finder owned the vein and could follow it beyond the vertical line of his claim. This freedom to make a claim encouraged miners to try their luck. Otherwise, many would not have made the effort.

Agriculturally, the gold rush meant an extension of the frontier up to, over, and down the Rocky Mountains. And this development in turn stimulated lines of transcontinental communication and transportation. People and goods had to get to California. Messages had to be sent there and back. The overland stages, the pony express, the telegraph, and the railroad eventually linked the East with the West.

The stimulus the gold rush provided to the growth of San Francisco, California, the West, and the United States extended to other nations and to the capitalist system as a whole. The coincidence that Karl Marx and Friedrich Engels published the *Communist Manifesto* in London in the year of the gold discovery, illustrates the need for caution in forecasting economic events.

The capitalist system of free enterprise was boosted by the California gold rush. It also helped the gold standard, despite early fears that the price of gold would slump. The gold standard, then operated by Britain, was later accepted by other nations. From the 1870s, gold was the basis of financing international trade and payments.

The impact of the gold rush on other countries varied enormously. Those most affected were in the process of development. Nations such as Chile and Peru, with a long history, were helped economically by the gold rush, as were the United States and European countries. Politically, too, the freedom of the gold seekers stimulated political dissatisfaction with conservative governments.

Yet the developing nations, such as Australia and New Zealand, probably were more greatly affected. Chance played a role. Many forty-niners must have noticed that gold was found in certain types of rocks. Some were reminded of similar rocks back home. Edward Hammond Hargraves from Australia was one such observer. He went back to Australia and is credited with starting the Australian gold rush of 1851. Australia gained in wealth and population. Ripples from this gold rush spread to New Zealand and Chile, both nations very much interested in exporting foodstuffs.

The gold rush and the establishment of mining in the West had later consequences for the United States during the Civil War. The Union had many uneasy moments raising money. California gold and Nevada silver helped out. Just how great the relative contribution was is hard to judge, since by then the gold output of California had fallen sharply.

One estimate gives a total from California and Nevada combined of $3,000,000 or $4,000,000 monthly. That may not sound very much, but it would have come to over $150,000,000 in the course of the war. Prices were much lower then, and the population much smaller. A similar impact today would require several billion dollars.

The California gold rush was clearly an event of national and international importance. For the world's common man, it was a liberation from poverty and squalor, an indication that all men were potentially equal when all had the same chance. For the United States, it meant the linking of the East with the West. For California, it was the beginning of the modern age. Few events in history have had so great an impact as the 1848 discovery of gold in the foothills of the Sierra.

12

WHAT DID THE GOLD RUSH ACHIEVE?

Accurate statistics on California's early years are not available, although many estimates have been made. Assessing them is also difficult, for several reasons. Intangibles, for instance, play a great role in economic development. A sense of opportunity, which is what the gold rush provided, gave California a boost that it still enjoys.

Yet the tangibles, such as gold output, present their own problems, since we have no exact figures, the population of California then was small, and the price of gold has risen enormously.

During the gold rush, gold was worth $18 an ounce. Because the silver content reduced the value of gold found in the goldfields, nuggets and gold dust were worth less than that. Just how much was paid depended on various factors, such as the normal ones of supply and demand. Sellers anxious to sell could do badly, especially in the 1848 rush when considerable amounts of gold were found and the gold-buying trade was not well organized. Later, sellers would receive something like the price offered by the Philadelphia mint, or $18 an ounce less service charges.

For nearly a century following the gold rush, gold sold for not much more than the $18 price, even though other prices had risen sharply. The gradual devaluation of the dollar in 1933 and 1934 boosted the price of gold from around $21 an ounce to $35, at which level it stayed for nearly forty years. Then, following an international financial crisis, the price of gold was allowed to rise on what was called the free market as opposed to the official price. The result was an increase in the early 1970s of some 400 percent in the price of gold in two or three years. That made it ten times more valuable than in 1848 and during the gold rush.

This vast difference makes comparisons with 1848 difficult. Either we take the $18 price of gold and think of it in terms of other prices in 1848. Or we take the current price of gold and consider it in relation to other current prices. We must also, of course, make allowance for the very small population of California in the gold rush years.

The net result is a very impressive showing for gold's impact on California. Before 1847, gold output in all of California's history was not more than $8,000 at the $18-an-ounce price. Obviously, gold was of trivial importance up to the gold rush years.

In the decade 1848–1857, at least $400,000,000 in gold was produced in California. Obviously, much of the production must have gone unrecorded. How much can only be guessed, since miners took gold home with them, sold it in the East, or kept it as a memento. Not all the gold was sold to the gold buyers who rushed to the scene.

The best year was 1852. At that time, the 1849 gold rush craze was fading. Companies with much capital and expensive equipment had moved in. The day of the solitary miner was largely over. In that year alone, over $80,000,000 of gold was produced at the $18 price. Multiply by ten to get some idea of the true impact in today's terms, and you will get a figure of nearly a billion dollars.

Such a sum would be significant in California even today.

In 1852, the impact on a much smaller population must have been tremendous. California clearly jumped ahead from a golden base.

Thousands of miners shared the pickings. They fared variously, some picking up a fortune and making off with it, others dying in the attempt. In 1849, average earnings may have been from $400 to $600 at the $18-an-ounce price for gold. Multiply by ten, and we get approximately $5,000 in today's terms, hardly rich pay for a year's hard grind in the expensive wilds. Yet the opportunity to earn that amount and have a chance of making a fortune would still make the opportunity acceptable to millions of people, especially those living in countries with a low standard of living.

Population figures are equally hard to come by. We may say, broadly speaking, that few Americans were living in California when gold was discovered, and that most of the arrivals in the next decade came to look for gold or engage in trade based on gold.

The population became heavily male. In 1850, about 8 percent of California's population was female. In the mining camps, it was about 2 percent. Over 70 percent of the males were between twenty and forty years of age.

The gold rush soon transformed Mexico's California into an American-dominated society. Most of the gold seekers were American, even though others came from the ends of the earth. Various pressures against foreigners, including discriminatory taxation, compelled many of them to go back home, thus reinforcing the grip that Americans had achieved by their victory over Mexico and the large influx of American gold seekers.

By the end of 1851, most of those from Mexico, Chile, and Peru had returned home. To some extent, they had been replaced by a vast influx of Chinese.

The sharp rise in population lasted until about 1853; then the rate of growth fell sharply although the population continued to rise. Foreign immigrants continued to arrive in considerable numbers, while Americans from the East became less important. The result was a rise in the percentage of foreign-born living in California.

A very rough guide is given by the following estimates. The non-Indian population of California rose dramatically after the summer of 1848. By December, some 6,000 Americans were living in California. By July 1849, their numbers had grown to 15,000, and by December 1849 to 53,000. In September 1850, the white population of California was around 93,000, and probably over 100,000 at the end of 1850. In 1852, California's population was some 220,000, and in the spring of 1853 around 300,000. By 1860, about 380,000 were living in California, 40 percent being foreign-born. The black population was then about 4,000. The Chinese numbered some 35,000 in 1860, up from 20,000 in 1852. The Irish accounted for about 33,000, the Germans about 22,000, and the British some 16,000. Other foreign national groups were sharply lower.

The main city to gain by the gold rush, of course, was San Francisco, the port of entry for tens of thousands and the destination of many from the East. From a small settlement of less than a thousand souls early in 1848, San Francisco had grown into a major city and international port with a population of 40,000 in 1850.

California and San Francisco in those early years were clearly dominated by gold, since there was almost nothing else in the whole of the state. The individual miner, however, fared less well, since the work was hard and lonesome and part if not most of what he earned was spent on goods and services at very high prices. By and large, the life was grinding and poorly rewarding in terms of what could be bought by the proceeds. Cold economic terms, however, are clearly an inadequate measure of the California gold rush. They do not take into account human emotions, or deal with a tide of people flooding a promised land, or with the development of a

new state that completed the acquisition by Americans of a continent to be dominated by the United States.

Today, when we say gold rush we think of California. So do millions outside the United States. We do not think in terms of how much gold was extracted or how many miners became wealthy. We know in our bones that these facts matter little.

We become more interested when we realize that California gold made a significant contribution to the Civil War of 1861–1865. We appreciate history more when we know that Dana the mineralogist, Sherman the soldier, and Wilkes the sailor, among many others, spent some time in California in those early years.

In brief, the California gold rush is a human epic, to be measured not in dollars and gold, but in terms of national development, international repercussions, the growth of the West, the making of the United States, and the mass migration of men and women to a new land.

If we must judge the gold rush in financial terms, we must assess it a great success for California, but a failure, in those gold rush years of 1849–1853, for many if not most of the gold seekers. How many goldbugs later turned to other forms of mining, trade and agriculture in California we do not know. Some stayed. Others left for parts unknown.

What we do know is that by the mere act of going to seek gold they formed part of one of the world's most famous and emotional events.

PART TWO

FOR DISCUSSION

13

WAS JAMES K. POLK
A GREAT PRESIDENT?

We live in an age of fallen idols. Cynicism abounds. Few people nowadays are regarded as great. Yet history is dotted with individuals who are commonly referred to as "great." Could this be because their actions, behavior, or courage produced great results, such as putting a nation on a new course, or paving the way for massive consequences for the human race?

Certainly we all know that a nation needs leadership, that this country has survived because leadership was there when it was needed. We also know that history is often very selective, that famous men and women who did great deeds are somehow forgotten. Sometimes we remember the event but not the participants. We recall the gold rush, but how about the man who was President during it?

Does it matter? Yes, unless we take it for granted that what happened in the course of this nation's history was automatically bound to occur in the way it did, no matter who led the country.

History obviously has not been kind to the eleventh President of the United States, James Knox Polk, Democrat. To many, his name is either unknown or dimly recalls the era before the Civil War. To others, he falls under the shadows of two more highly regarded Presidents, Andrew Jackson, Democrat, his political hero, and Abraham Lincoln, Republican.

Also, Polk is outside the age of modern politics with its Republican and Democratic political parties. In his day, there were Democrats, Whigs (the successors of the Federalists), and some minor parties. The Democrats dominated national life from 1801 to 1861, even though they did not win all the presidential elections. The Republican party was founded only in 1854–1856.

President Polk is often regarded as the first "dark horse" of presidential politics, since he was little known in the country at large, and was the compromise candidate in 1844. Yet he was well known in Tennessee politics and in the nation's capital.

Early in his political life, Polk acquired the nickname of Napoleon of the Stump, since he was of short stature, like Napoleon, but a popular orator. His friendship with President Andrew Jackson, also from Tennessee, a gentleman known as Old Hickory from his toughness, gave Polk another nickname, Young Hickory. But Polk was in and out of the general national consciousness in a few short years—five or six at most. He retired in 1849 after one term, as he had promised to do on election, and died a few months later, from cholera and from the general exhaustion of the presidential office.

Few liberals have ever thought highly of Polk. He was from the South, North Carolina, and lived in Tennessee, then the West. He did not concern himself with grave social problems, and favored westward expansion, to the dismay of those who felt that it would mean the extension of slavery into new territory.

Nor did Polk commend himself generally by his austere mode of life, his inflexible integrity, and his lack of social charm. His war against Mexico was sharply criticized at the time, and has been even more so since. The philosophy of Manifest Destiny, which he firmly espoused, has never endeared Polk to liberal thinkers. In general, President Polk has been ignored by biographers, and he remains today largely unknown.

Yet objective analysis suggests that this man of considerable ability was a good President. Some historians rate him highly. President Harry S. Truman felt that Polk had been badly misjudged by history. Because Polk is the central political figure in the story of the California gold rush, we would be wise to examine his record in greater detail. He is shown below in a list of Presidents from 1829 to 1865.

7th	Andrew Jackson	Democrat	1829–1837
8th	Martin Van Buren	Democrat	1837–1841
9th	William Henry Harrison	Whig	1841
10th	John Tyler	Whig	1841–1845
11th	James Knox Polk	Democrat	1845–1849
12th	Zachary Taylor	Whig	1849–1850
13th	Millard Fillmore	Whig	1850–1853
14th	Franklin Pierce	Democrat	1853–1857
15th	James Buchanan	Democrat	1857–1861
16th	Abraham Lincoln	Republican	1861–1865

Polk was clearly neither preceded nor followed by great Presidents. That may have been due in part to the problems then facing the nation. The Whigs, for instance, were split over the question of slavery into Northern and Southern Whigs. The Democrats usually prevailed, even though the Whigs elected Presidents in 1840 and 1848. The national moral confusion over westward expansion and slavery generated few political leaders of stature, probably because national selfish interests in expansion and sectional selfish interests in slavery overwhelmed moral considerations.

Polk had other things than slavery on his mind. He formulated four main goals for his announced four-year presidency. These were the reduction of import duties or tariffs, the reestablishment of an independent Treasury (as opposed to private banks) for the deposit of federal funds, the settlement of the Oregon country dispute with Britain, and the acquisition of California.

Polk, a man of discipline, achieved them all, which puts him next after President George Washington as a successful President. Polk's presidency was the best for territorial expansion. Texas became a state in 1845, Iowa in 1846, and Wisconsin in 1848. Oregon became a territory in 1848, and Minnesota in 1849.

President Polk knew what he wanted and how to get it. His experience as Congressman and as Speaker of the House of Representatives was useful in his relations with the Congress. Indeed, he is the only Speaker ever to become President.

His toughness combined with integrity to produce a formidable opponent, as foreign powers discovered, yet his desire for westward expansion and the acquisition of the then independent Texas, plus a good chunk of the Oregon country, did not overrule his sense of what was reasonable and acceptable in the field of foreign relations.

Thus while he annexed Texas and defeated Mexico in the 1846–1848 war, Polk did not completely demolish that country. He took only the northerly third, which was largely unoccupied except for Americans. A similar reasonableness applied to his attitude on the Oregon country boundary. Polk agreed with Britain that it should be on the 49th parallel, in spite of the "Fifty-four-forty or fight" slogan with which his election campaign had been fought.

Today, when we look at the map of the United States, we think, partly because we are so accustomed to seeing it, that the boundaries of the continental United States look fair and reasonable. Yet the results could have been far different. The United States could easily have been in a much less advantageous position. President Polk saw to it that the boundaries, by and large, favored this nation.

The area that Polk acquired for the United States was huge. Mexico, for instance, gave up all claims to Texas, and the United States acquired the whole or part of what are now Arizona, California, Colorado, Nevada, New Mexico, Utah, and Wyoming—surely a fabulous achievement in the "fabulous forties."

Those were the exciting days of the Oregon Trail, the new telegraph system, the California gold rush, and expansion. Yet the United States population in 1848 was less than 23,000,000.

Within a decade or so of Polk's death in 1849, the old Whig party had disappeared, the new Republican party had been formed, and the Democrats, like their Whig opponents before them, had split into two parties, one in the South and one in the North, paving the way for the victory of Abraham Lincoln, once a Whig but now a Republican.

We see Lincoln, of course, every time we look at that period in American history. Seldom do we catch a glance of Polk. The tragedy of the Civil War overshadows everything else. We must ask: To what extent was President Polk responsible for the Civil War?

As a southerner and a westerner, Polk felt at home with slavery and favored expansion. Both attitudes stemmed from his personal experience. Basically, he could not visualize national life without slavery and westward expansion. The South was so dependent on slavery that Polk naturally supported it.

As one who had migrated westward, Polk believed that destiny had made manifest its intentions: the United States had to carve out a nation from the Atlantic to the Pacific, certainly the best slice of land in the world. Today, we take this for granted and forget Polk. We still wonder about the Civil War. We ask ourselves if it could possibly have been avoided.

Polk was concerned about matters that he thought major. He was worried about losing California. He thought that settlers in California might join with those in the Oregon country to proclaim an independent nation, calling it the California or Pacific Republic.

95

In Polk's day, a civil war over slavery was hardly expected—although it was feared by some. In this sense, Polk escapes the greater criticism leveled against those Presidents who immediately preceded Abraham Lincoln—Fillmore, Pierce, and Buchanan.

Assessing Polk as a President requires an understanding of the spirit of the times, of what was politically possible and nationally acceptable. The splits that occurred in the old Whig party and the Democratic party prove that slavery was the most momentous issue of that era. Westward expansion, of course, was intimately tied up with the slavery question, since northerners objected to creating new slave states. Even here, slavery generated the strongest emotions.

During Polk's political life, the United States was never in danger, as it was under other Presidents, such as George Washington and Franklin D. Roosevelt. The nation obviously could handle Mexico. Great Britain, controlling Canada, had no illusions that it could reconquer the United States. Polk, therefore, was free from major foreign pressures. He made sure nothing would change that by agreeing with Britain over the Oregon boundary. That left Mexico—an easy target for the United States.

Polk's main interests were clearly expansionism in two areas, territory and trade, for both of which finances were needed. His achievements in his four years as President can be summed up in four words: tariffs, Treasury, Oregon, California. Even two would suffice: territory, finance.

President Polk might thus be described as successful but limited. He does not achieve greatness because his presidency neither decided a moral issue nor protected the United States against a foreign foe.

Nor is Polk ever likely to be regarded as a great President. Revisionism, or a new look at former Presidents, can go only so far. Polk completed the map of the United States and made the shape of the nation what it is today. He set out what he wished to do and did it well. We may perhaps excuse him for not putting a greater emphasis on the slave issue and other social problems, since all of us are limited and can reasonably attempt only so much. A wise man knows his limitations.

Polk, like all of us, was the product of his experience. He never transcended it. He was a southerner accustomed to if not attached to slavery. He was a westerner out in Tennessee who believed that the nation should expand to the Pacific within fairly regular boundaries. His other interests were trade and finance.

Today, these matters still concern us but they do not excite us. Emotions have always been stronger than either land or money. The slavery issue provided the real emotion in Polk's day, just as racial and other forms of discrimination do today. We can rate President Polk as successful, reasonable, wise, and just—but limited. He failed to take a stand on the great emotional problem of the day, slavery. He was never expected to do so. He could not have been expected to do so. Without it, however, Polk could never be anything but a very competent President, not a great one.

14

WAS MANIFEST DESTINY A VALID MORAL CONCEPT?

Concepts take on new meaning as the years pass. How has Manifest Destiny fared? What lessons can be learned from its application by the United States? Is it completely discredited? Was it ever truly valid?

We have seen how the term came into being in a magazine article in July 1845, and how it became popular when it was repeated in a newspaper in December 1845. For decades, Manifest Destiny served well all those who believed in American expansionism from coast to coast and from north to south.

The coining of the expression, of course, was but the formal ratification of thoughts and ideas of long standing. The phrase came into being when the United States needed a concise expression of national will, determination, and desire.

In 1845, the nation had all the land it could use for its current population. Even if all today's population were concentrated in the space occupied by the United States in 1845, the country would be far less populous than many others today. So there was land enough and to spare in 1845.

Yet many did not then think so, since the land acquired by

the Louisiana Purchase of 1803 had been settled in part, and the territory later to be forcibly acquired from Mexico by the war of 1846–1848 was not yet under American control.

The Industrial Revolution born in Britain in the previous century was sweeping not only over Europe but over the United States as well. Industrialists felt the need for expansion, for more land and bigger markets. The vast technological changes brought about by the railroad, the telegraph, the steamship, and numerous other inventions and ideas made people confident in the future of a United States that would roll from the Atlantic to the Pacific.

Unfortunately, some stumbling blocks were in the way. Mexico was one. Canada, a British territory, lay to the north. National interest seemed to demand that both nations, Canada and Mexico, get out of the way.

The nation was feverish for a time, demanding a big chunk of the Oregon country from Britain, and war with Mexico. Since both matters came to be settled almost simultaneously, some claimed that land was lost to Canada. Mexico gave up the northerly third of its empire to the United States after a war opposed by many Americans, including Abraham Lincoln, then the lone Whig Congressman from Illinois, 1847–1849.

That was not the end of Manifest Destiny. Cuba in 1854 and the Philippines in 1898 generated similar cries of annexation for the benefit of the United States. In all cases, however, the United States avoided becoming a long-term colonial power. The land acquired from Mexico was sparsely settled, as was that in the Pacific Northwest to which Canada also had claims. Troubles arose over Cuba and the Philippines, but the United States wisely repudiated annexationist views.

Yet in the sweep of history we see that Manifest Destiny produced a certain mentality among Americans that generated trouble later. The belief that the world must be altered for the benefit of the United States gained hold, as did the assumption that all peoples would be far better off living as Americans do.

Certain ideas about the righteousness of national thinking were common long after Manifest Destiny had ceased to have any application within the continental frame of reference. Even today, many Americans feel that life in the United States is the best available and can be transplanted anywhere with a little effort.

Americans, of course, are not the only people who have suffered from a superiority complex. From time immemorial, peoples and nations have assumed superiority over others. The failing is common, since it pleases people to feel superior.

What we see, looking back on these pretensions, is their self-serving nature and arrogance. The world is full of ancient cities that have become digging sites for archeologists, forgotten about completely, or eking out a living as tourist attractions. Empires have come and gone. Once-famous settlements are now remembered mainly because of their fallen temples or golden objects.

Yet at one time or another, most of these cultures basked in the warmth of their self-congratulations. Their peoples believed they were superior to others. They were entitled to what others had. Their ends justified their means.

Can criticism of this nature be levied against the United States? What would North America be like without the Monroe Doctrine? Would it really matter very much if Texas and California were independent? Would it have been better to allow the Confederacy its independence?

We see the United States as one of three large nations occupying North America. Obviously, Manifest Destiny had its limitations. Otherwise, the United States would occupy all of North America. Similar conditions exist elsewhere, even where geography seems to favor political unity. In Europe, for instance, the Iberian Peninsula is occupied by Spain and Portugal. South America is split into a dozen or more independent nations. How many nations make up Africa? Does it really matter?

What Manifest Destiny teaches us is that arguments are made to suit a purpose. Putting it differently, we see ourselves as eminently reasonable if we can find sophistry that justifies our needs. Manifest Destiny became gospel for millions, since it invoked divine inevitability in the interests of the United States. What many Americans wanted was so beyond anything reasonable that destiny—Manifest Destiny—had to be summoned to their aid.

Was it all deceit? No. The splitting up of continents, even islands, into independent nations stems from various historical developments over the centuries. Spain and Portugal, for instance, so ran their colonies in South America that they became separate nations on independence. The separate American colonies of North America, controlled by Britain, joined into a nation in 1776 because of the nature of British rule.

Once founded, the United States and its citizens naturally moved west. The colonists had done that right from the beginning, and the trend continued. In this way, American settlers came up against American Indians, Canadians, and Mexicans. By and large, all were swept out of the way. The result is a United States that today almost looks like the work, one might say, of Manifest Destiny.

Except for Alaska and Hawaii, and a few chunks of other territory here and there, the United States seems almost manifestly destined to be one nation.

Yet several flaws can be found in this argument. Obviously, Manifest Destiny came up against the reality of others' rights. Mexico was defeated, but only so much territory could reasonably be taken from it. Otherwise, the United States would have become a colonial power with many problems. Canada, under Britain, would have fought the United States had not a reasonable view been taken by President Polk.

Also, Manifest Destiny puts a nation above international

law. That may suit a nation well in one or more particular cases, but does any nation wish to live constantly without international law? If not, why should not international law apply to all cases, not just some?

Another flaw is that others can use the same argument of Manifest Destiny. Canada, for instance, was expanding westward, as was the United States. Any Canadian Manifest Destiny might have clashed with American views, and would have been denounced as self-serving and greedy.

The lesson to be learned from the American experience of Manifest Destiny is that such arguments can be dangerous, even though sophistry is common in personal, social, professional, and business life, as well as in national affairs.

The United States has been fortunate in acquiring such a magnificent slice of territory while avoiding major colonial obligations. Wisdom as well as luck played a role, of course. Often enough, as with Mexico, the United States drew back from acquiring territory that could cause trouble later.

Also, the very structure of the Constitution of the United States enabled it to absorb, without too much trouble, territory, such as Hawaii, that had a very different history from the rest of the nation.

For the most part, however, Manifest Destiny applied to the continental United States and has been limited within that territory to land not settled in any meaningful way by others. That was wise, since the problems faced by the United States in minority-race matters suggest that acquisition of colonial territory might have been disastrous.

That, perhaps, is the major lesson to be drawn from the nation's experience with Manifest Destiny. It worked as well as it did because it was a limited Manifest Destiny that justified the taking over of land not heavily populated.

Manifest Destiny was clearly an easy slogan to live with in the middle decades of the nineteenth century. In practice, of course, it had to be modified to meet the realities of the situation. Yet it never sank completely out of sight. Even after the

United States had occupied most of its present continental territory, the thinking behind Manifest Destiny kept cropping up as new situations arose that justified its resurrection.

Facile arguments that so easily serve the nation's self-interest should be carefully scrutinized at all times, especially when the sophistry invokes the Deity. Other nations have their own deities. And often, when deities conflict, wars erupt.

15

WHY DID SOME NATIONS
FEAR THE GOLD RUSH?

The California gold discovery of 1848 was not welcome everywhere, especially as the 1849 gold rush developed. Many hostile views were expressed at home and abroad.

Great Britain, for instance, was then the only major nation on the gold standard. That is, its currency was linked directly to gold at a fixed rate of exchange. Other nations used a system of bimetallism under which gold and silver were maintained at a fixed ratio. Usually, gold was worth sixteen or sixteen and a half times as much as silver.

In those days, gold was extremely important, nationally and in international finance. That had long been the case. Following the opening up of Central and South America after Columbus, and the sacking of palaces, temples, and graves, gold and golden objects and silver flooded Europe, causing inflation and economic dislocation.

The use of cheap or slave labor in Spanish America to produce gold also had financial and political repercussions in Europe. Gold was simply another word for currency. A vast influx of it meant a big increase in the money supply, hence inflation, since more money was chasing the available goods.

Gold also meant power. In those days, a nation with gold deposits was similar to oil-rich countries today, or even to major gold producers today, such as South Africa. That was shown later, in the Civil War, when gold from a loyal California and silver from a loyal Nevada helped finance the Union armies. Gold in California meant that the United States had become that more powerful and important, a greater force in economic competition and foreign trade.

It meant more than that. California faces the Pacific. Not only had a new, rich part of the United States suddenly arisen that joined up with the eastern United States facing the Atlantic, but the United States now was a Pacific power and obviously meant to stay that way. Beneath the gold-rush jokes from Britain were real fears that the United States had become that much more significant.

Britain had many interests abroad. One such, of course, was Canada. The war of 1812–1814 with the United States had been fought mainly over Canada, and neither Britain nor Canada knew what impact Californian gold would have on international relations. Certainly, the United States gained relative to Canada and Britain.

Chile was another power that viewed askance the abundance of gold in California. Chile, then the most important Pacific nation, must have felt that California would soon be a rival for international trade.

Australia, another land controlled by Britain, was affected adversely by the gold rush, even though it later gained when Californian miners participated in the Australian gold rush of 1851. Many Australians tried to prevent the migration of gold seekers to California. They argued that Australia needed all the men it could get, that a labor shortage would raise wages, and that labor would become more powerful politically.

The resentment against California was not confined to foreign countries. Many states in the United States feared the impact of the gold rush. Michigan complained that money was being taken out of the state as well as emigrants.

105

People were mortgaging their farms or selling them outright to get funds for the overland trip. Employers in other states felt the loss of young men who dashed off to the mines.

Still another factor causing concern was the newness of the California gold rush. Nothing like it had ever happened before. The newness itself was disturbing, tending to excite ridicule. Fancy picking up gold!

During the Middle Ages, European gold came from the mines of Saxony and Austria and some from Spain, but these deposits were not open to the general public. The idea that any Tom, Dick, or Harry could rush off to California to pan for gold, even to pick up nuggets or small boulders of gold, seemed most laughable—yet worrisome. If this could happen, anything could!

The problem of massive migrations also caused concern. Britain, for instance, has always been a land of emigrants, but most have always gone to what were called Empire or Commonwealth countries. California gold was a real threat to this emigration to British lands overseas. Emigrants in Britain were encouraged to Try Canada First!

The loss of population was a threat even in itself to some nations. Ireland, then one nation governed from London as part of the United Kingdom of Britain and Ireland, had already lost millions from the potato famine. Now, gold in California was beckoning! Cholera in Britain also had killed thousands and had affected business and trade.

In continental Europe, revolution or change of one variety or another had long been in the air in France, Germany, Austria, and Italy. Gold for the picking in California could only worsen labor discontent. How could factories be run if workers emigrated to the diggings for better rewards, even fortunes?

Germany was particularly concerned, since it was belatedly but rapidly changing from an agricultural to a highly industrialized society. The last thing it wanted was inflation and labor unrest! Trade had been badly hurt by the revolution of

1848 and the subsequent counterrevolution. The growing migration to California would not help produce contentment in the factories.

France and Italy, although politically troubled, were not so badly affected by emigration to California. France may even have welcomed it, partly out of the long friendship with the United States, and partly out of the hope that some of the troublemakers in France would find gold and San Francisco more attractive than creating revolutions in Paris. On balance, however, France and such countries as Canada and those in Latin America probably did not relish this extra advantage for the United States coming from California gold.

The California gold rush, of course, was seen by other nations against the background of recent events. These included the revolutions in Europe, which indicated rapid change in social and political structures following industrialization, the recent victory of the United States over Mexico, and the fairly recent loss by Spain and Portugal of most of their overseas empires. Europe seemed to be coming apart at the seams just as the United States was bursting its bounds.

The democratic way of life in the United States had already made many Europeans uneasy. Californian gold, they thought, would produce even greater social leveling, which could spread across the Atlantic even as the American Revolution of 1776 had done.

Envy also played a role in attitudes. The United States, which had just acquired California from Mexico, was expected to gain a modest amount from the hide and tallow trade. But here was gold instead of grease!

Most of the fears, of course, were never realized. Indeed, cooler heads at the time suggested that the world as a whole would benefit from California gold. The London *Economist,* for instance, discounted the belief that gold was in danger from overproduction, or that serious damage to international trade would result. The opposite, argued the *Economist.*

The discovery of gold in California actually boosted the international esteem of gold after the first shock subsided. Capitalism, or free enterprise, got a shot in the arm even as Karl Marx and Friedrich Engels were publishing the *Communist Manifesto*. The English-speaking world gained instead of losing.

Still, the California gold rush, coming when it did, was a great shock to many. One can easily see why. It was new. It disturbed established thinking. It encouraged human freedom when the Old Guard was already fearful. It boosted the United States both in wealth and manpower, linking the East and West. It was just another indication that the power that Europe had maintained for centuries was quickly slipping across the Atlantic, even to the Pacific.

16

IS DISCRIMINATION EVER JUSTIFIED?

The California gold rush produced many forms of discrimination, all of them ugly. Gold was at stake. So were jobs, land, and capital. Desperate men do desperate deeds. Fear breeds crime. The goldfields of California, as well as the early coastal and inland settlements, saw more than their fair share of discrimination, racial and otherwise, and of injustice.

Discrimination in more than one variety has long been a serious moral problem in the United States. It came to this land in the minds of the colonists who first settled these shores in the seventeenth century. They were the victims of discrimination, yet they could not avoid using it to their own advantage, even though they resented its use against themselves.

Religious bigotry was part and parcel of their intellectual baggage. Racial discrimination here began with the importation of slave labor by these early colonists, many of whom had fled from gross political and religious oppression and economic servitude to a land of opportunity in the New World. Yet because the slave trade and slavery were accepted features of international life at that time, the use of black labor—to give the white settlers a better standard of living—was accepted without too much thought.

Thus there grew up in the American colonies an accepted distinction between those with white and those with non-white faces. The existence of red-skinned American Indians, of course, merely emphasized—even proved, to their way of thinking—that a white skin was the gift of God and conferred the right to lord it over those of darker hues.

This distinction deriving from skin color, however, is not limited to whites. Until the middle of the nineteenth century, for instance, the Japanese and Chinese regarded those with white skins as barbarians. "Celestials" was the name the Chinese gave themselves. They resisted white trading settlements in their country. The Japanese used to fire on ships containing white people that approached their shores. Obviously, they wished to be left alone.

Fear of something different—even simple fear—is probably one reason for this ancient form of discrimination. Another is economic gain from using others as slaves, or from limiting educational or job opportunities. But is something else involved? Is there a basic need among humans to create distinctions that confer superiority on some and disadvantages on others? So widespread is discrimination in one form or another all over the world, that it seems at times almost a natural part of life.

Does discrimination serve any useful social purpose? The United States, for instance, has long been criticized for its racial attitudes. Other nations, such as South Africa and Rhodesia, have fared worse. In countries such as the United States, South Africa, and Rhodesia, the major distinction is clearly between black and white skins.

Yet other countries have a similar problem in class consciousness. Britain, even with its post-1945 immigration from India, Pakistan, Africa, and the West Indies, is still a highly homogeneous nation. About 90 percent of its people are white Protestants, with non-whites, Roman Catholics, and Jews forming the balance. Yet to many observers, Britain is highly class-conscious. The whites have long been stratified into social classes that have been maintained despite relative affluence and a welfare state.

It may even be argued that the slight ebbing of class consciousness in Britain in the last few decades stems as much from the influx of nonwhite skins as from any genuine improvement of feeling among class-conscious whites.

Many new nations faced serious problems with the indigenous or original native occupants. The American Indian, of course, concerns us in the United States as in other nations of North and South America. Australia had aborigines and New Zealand the Maoris. New Zealand fared reasonably well in its racial problems. Australia has made great efforts in the recent past to compensate for its early bad treatment of the aborigines.

What we find generally is that nations and people are ashamed of, and usually on the defensive about, all forms of discrimination. Cynics may argue that this does not prevent new devices to maintain discrimination. Others may fairly point out that generosity usually must come after financial security for oneself and family has been assured.

Thus white Australians made sure the continent was theirs before dealing more generously with the aborigines. The United States took a good part of the North American continent before seeking to deal fairly with the American Indians. Other nations have similar histories.

The validity of this argument can be seen from general observation. Nations, like people, look after their own interests. They find justification in all sorts of arguments and rationalizations. Economic matters, basically the standard of living, are the cause of much of the trouble. Differences in education, employment, and income are found in racially troubled and other societies.

The distinction between black and white, for instance, enables white South Africans to have a fairly high standard of living based on cheap black labor. In many industrialized countries of Europe, the boy or girl from an industrial worker's family has only a poor chance of obtaining a college education or a good job, unless the family is smaller than average.

We see here how racial consciousness and class consciousness spring from the same causes. Religion and ethnic background also have been used to create distinctions. Yet a society can tolerate only so much division within itself.

Social stratification among white Australians is possible, since there are so few nonwhite Australians. The general lack of social strata among South African whites, even though they are of Dutch and British descent, reflects the need for white unity against the nonwhite majority.

Races and classes get together in harmony when the need arises. Otherwise, that is, when the need is not great, racial and class differences tend to create distinctions that confer privileges on some and disadvantages on others.

The racial and class divisions in the United States, as elsewhere, unfortunately have long historical roots that have enabled discrimination to exist in one form or another for centuries. Fortunately, although progress often seems slow, the situation is improving throughout the world, possibly because of rising living standards and better educational opportunities.

The ugliness of the discrimination that existed in the California gold rush appears shocking today, but the basically selfish and fearful nature of all types of discrimination can be seen clearly if we examine the history of civilization. From a race, class, or personal viewpoint, discrimination can be justified on grounds of greed, but it has no ethical base. In the long run—indeed, even in the short run—it serves no useful national purpose.

In fact, the opposite applies, for talent is wasted and national energies are consumed in dealing with social strife, resentment, and bitterness.

Discrimination, however, will long be with us. A nation has only so much wealth, only so many educational opportunities, only so many good jobs. The discrimination we see today has long links to that original slavery going back thousands of years. Little actual slavery exists today, but discrimination abounds all over the world. Morally, it is as objectionable as the slave trade and slavery. It has no more justification today than it did in the days of the gold rush.

17

SUPPOSE THERE HAD BEEN NO GOLD RUSH

Suppose gold had never been discovered in California? What then? The gigantic international migration would never have occurred. The development of the state would have proceeded more slowly. The north, especially San Francisco, would not have leapt into prominence. The south would have grown in step with the north, possibly faster. The lawlessness that characterized the early years probably would have been absent. The leisurely cattle and farming economy would have gradually absorbed the newcomers already traveling overland from the East.

Few migrants would have bothered going to California around Cape Horn, or via the Isthmus of Panama. The American Indians, the Chinese, and others with nonwhite skins would have suffered less injustice. The growth of California's cities, instead of being frantic, almost chaotic, would have proceeded in more orderly fashion. The transcontinental railroad would have been completed later than it was.

Today, California would be a different place. Just how different, it is hard to guess. The Mexican War had already been won by the United States when gold was discovered.

California then was part of American territory. Today, gold or no gold, California would be a prosperous state with a big population.

That was almost inevitable from the start. California had much more than gold to offer, but the 1848 discovery put on the state the golden stamp. California acquired a certain style of life, certain attitudes, and developed in the way it did because of gold. Gold was the state's hallmark.

Rushes for gold have occurred elsewhere. Often they made a huge difference, as in Australia and South Africa. Elsewhere, the impact of a rush, whether for gold, silver, or diamonds, was less marked. Some places boomed, then became deserted mining camps and ghost towns.

That happened in California also. Many forty-niners simply got disgusted and left. Some stayed. More came. Many prospered in something other than gold. Cattle raising, tallow, and hides had long provided the base of the economy. Trade, local and overseas, and a growing industry and agriculture could be built on that.

Today, a similar gold rush in California would have relatively little impact. In 1848–1849, California was being formed. The state was Spanish-speaking and Roman Catholic. It soon became English-speaking and substantially Protestant. Gold made California famous. Earlier, most people could not have found California on a map. The question "Where's California?" changed in essence to the exclamation "California, here I come!"

The gold rush attracted many people with considerable skills. Mining quickly put an emphasis on education and intelligence. From cattle on pasture, the emphasis switched to mining. Later, crops took over, also making California famous.

California had many advantages from the start, including its location on the Pacific coast. The covered wagons had to stop there. They had started to arrive before the gold rush, and kept on coming in droves for two more decades until the transcontinental railroad was finished in 1869.

Most of these newcomers would have gone to California, gold or no gold. Gold quickly lost its public allure. Essentially, it was a shot in the arm that boosted California in a few years from a sleepy outlying province into a land that all the world talked about.

Had California been a barren land, as it was and still is in parts, the gold would have stimulated an economy that could not have supported many people for long. The other states on the West Coast, Oregon and Washington, developed quite differently. Gold, and obvious differences in climate, played a major role in California's relatively exotic growth.

Gold was important, since so many decisions in life stem from many factors. Gold put California in men's minds and hopes. Gold must have made the difference to many migrants for decades to come. California's natural resources, favorable location for world trade, climate, and scenery would have become known worldwide without the gold. The news spread by Yankee traders, who visited California long before 1848, had helped stimulate westward migration. Gold turned a national march west into a feverish scramble to get there fast—from all points on the globe. California has not lost that magnetism.

Gold made certain that California stayed American. The early belief that Yankees and Uncle Sam had concocted rumors of gold just to get people to go to California was wrong, of course. Yet the reasoning was not unreasonable.

President James K. Polk on taking office had determined to acquire California. No wonder he gloated over gold and spoke of its abundance. Polk did not live to see much of the gold rush, but he felt the need to acquire California to prevent the setting up of an independent republic along the Pacific. That could have happened but for gold.

Russia, of course, then possessed Alaska. Britain controlled Canada and claimed a huge chunk of what was then the Oregon country. Even though the Oregon question had been settled by 1848, the possibility—it was never a probability—existed that California would join with the Oregon country within the United States to form an independent republic. The West Coast might even have been split among Russia, Canada, and France. Gold prevented that. The world knew, after 1849, that the United States would fight hard to keep California.

Polk's fears of an independent California seem strange to us today. But they were reasonable then. Texas had been independent for a decade before joining the Union. Many Americans, in that age before the Mexican War, opposed westward expansion, especially if it meant war. They argued that slavery would be extended and become a permanent feature of American life, not just a peculiar institution in the cotton-growing Southeast.

What gold did to California was to make the West so important to the United States that the thought of allowing it to become independent just never occurred to anyone. Those who had opposed the Mexican War, those who had objected violently to the idea of taking over the wastes and deserts of the Southwest, those who had argued over the abolition of slavery, all fell strangely silent. What could they say? The gold of California made their arguments against westward expansion, on one ground or another, ridiculous. Gold had proved them wrong.

Once the forty-niners were on their way, the future of California as an important state of the Union was sealed. The huge boost given to the north and San Francisco at the expense of cities, such as Los Angeles, to the south, took decades to overcome. The rivalry still exists. San Francisco gradually changed from a boisterous youth into a city much more sedate, even conservative in many ways, especially in business. Los Angeles and the south eventually took over, partly for geographical and climatic reasons, the expansion that earlier occurred in the north.

Today, California has many great cities. Gold has long lost its importance as the major attraction. But the California gold rush is still the gold rush of world history. California began the legendary Golden West.

APPENDIX
THE LURE OF GOLD

The lure of gold has been known since time immemorial. Superlative examples of gold workmanship were produced by the Scythians, Egyptians, and other ancient peoples. Many of these works of art have come down to us almost in new condition. Their beauty leaves no doubt that the metal was highly esteemed, since the golden objects were found in the tombs of rulers.

The unusual nature of this lustrous yellow metal clearly made it immediately attractive to man. Its specific gravity, density, about seven times higher than the quartz rock or siliceous material in which it usually is found, put a nugget of gold among the curious natural objects picked up by migratory tribes as they wandered far and wide in search of grazing for their cattle. Gold's beauty, its unalterability, its occurrence in native or metallic condition, put it in a class by itself.

Even today, a genuine gold nugget is worth more than its weight in gold. The possession of a nugget, or object made of gold, brought joy to primitive peoples. The modern gold wedding band or ring serves a similar function.

Apparently, the world can never get enough gold. It has

long been accepted in return for goods and services. The alchemists of the Middle Ages spent their lives trying to convert base metals into gold. Today, we can do this by atomic bombardment, if we wish to spend the time and trouble, but the alchemists, peering through their fumes, were not so well informed. Fortunately, their efforts produced advances in chemistry other than the making of gold, so that their lives were not a total waste, even though most of them died disappointed.

Gold is simply one of the ninety or so chemical elements found in nature. It refuses to combine with most of the others. Hence, minerals or ores containing gold are few in number and limited in importance. Gold combines with other metals, such as silver, copper, and mercury, but not with the gases, such as oxygen, hydrogen, and nitrogen. This means that gold is untouched by water, air, or earth. Gold may remain in a tomb, earth bank, or river for centuries, yet remain pure.

Chemically pure gold, however, occurs very rarely in nature. Native or natural gold usually contains silver, even as much as 15 percent by weight. Most of the gold found in placer deposits, that is, those of sand, gravel, or earth in a bed, or former bed, of a stream, contains less silver than the gold recovered from primary deposits, such as veins in rocks. Surface weathering has removed some of the silver in placer gold, since silver, unlike gold, combines easily with many chemical elements, hence its tendency to tarnish. Gold with more than 15 percent silver is found, and is known as electrum.

Gold is very widely dispersed in the earth's crust and may be recovered from seawater. Gold's value makes mining operations possible even in deposits where gold is too finely dispersed to be seen, even on close examination. Gold is also recovered from copper and lead deposits. The so-called fool's gold, or pyrite, the yellow sulfide of iron, often contains small amounts of gold.

Gold's properties are truly remarkable. It has been beaten into gold leaf for thousands of years. Ancient Romans used this translucent material to add beauty to their buildings. Today, the space and defense programs find gold leaf useful, since it reflects up to 98 percent of incidental infrared radiation.

Gold, when alloyed with small amounts of silver and copper amounting to roughly 2 percent, that is, 23½-karat gold, may be worked to $1/280,000$ of an inch thick. Such gold leaf looks bluish-green as the light shines through it, a property known as bichromatism.

Gold leaf may also be reduced to a powder. Nature itself does this by constant abrasion over the centuries in stream beds. Many valuable deposits do not appear to contain any gold at all. Yet nuggets weighing hundreds of ounces have been collected. This contrast, between the possible fortune and the probable bits of impalpable powder or gold dust, accounts for much of gold's lure and consequent disappointment. The nuggets are the exception. Most of the gold recovered in history has come from deposits where the gold was not visible to the naked eye. An ounce of gold may be drawn into a wire fifty miles long. Nature, in effect, does the same. An ounce can be flattened into one hundred square feet.

Gold is recovered from two types of deposits, placer and lode. Geological changes sometimes turn the gravel of a placer deposit into a deep rock formation, or mix it with existing rocks or beds of slate. The gold found in California came from sand and gravel beds, decomposed granite, and intermixed with a kind of slate, which is simply a form of fine particles made solid by heat and pressure.

The placer or alluvial deposits were washed down by streams as they eroded the original gold-bearing rock. If the stream still uses the same bed, the placer is known as wet diggings. If the stream has meandered, leaving dried mud and gravel, the placer is called dry diggings.

The presence of water in wet diggings makes them easier

to work. Water has to be brought to dry diggings. If not, the mud has to be powdered and winnowed, as in separating chaff from grain. The heavy gold falls and is collected. The mud is supposed to get blown away. Often, some of the gold dust goes with it.

Wet diggings are operated similarly, but by using water instead of air to separate the heavy gold from the relatively lightweight mud, gravel, or crushed rock. Streams, of course, have been doing the same for ages. Nuggets of gold would sink into a crevice or hole in the bed of the stream, providing a bonanza for the lucky finder. Most of the gold was worn away into fine particles, powder, or flakes, mixed with the mud and gravel, and swirled downstream.

As the stream meandered, bars of mud formed on the bank opposite the turn, or bend, creating a form of plaza, hence the word placer. The forty-niners looked for these placers, in wet or dry form, and worked them. Or they tried their luck searching the stream bed for nuggets in crevices or hidden under boulders. The only other way to get gold was to trace the original vein in rock, dig it out, and crush it, making one's own alluvial deposit. Gold in slate was similar, except that the slate was itself dried mud, not original rock, such as a vein of quartz running through a hillside.

The forty-niners obviously had their work cut out for them if they were to be successful. They had to be lucky and find nuggets, or work hard and separate the fine gold from mud, slate, or quartz. Without luck, the work usually was desperately hard. The tales of fortunes picked up in stream beds were true enough, as was the news of rich placer deposits. Fickle nature had swept some huge nuggets into stream banks, or left them in stream beds. Placers varied enormously in richness, since some were nearer than others to the original source of the gold, while a few had grown rich in fine gold particles or flakes over the centuries.

The simplest task facing a forty-niner was digging mud, putting it into a receptacle, and washing it with water. The container usually used was a circular, flattish metal dish known as a pan, about a foot or so in diameter, with sloping sides that enabled water to run over easily. A wooden bowl with ridges, used similarly, was called a *batea*. Sometimes a tightly woven Indian basket was employed. Some miners were not above using an old boot. The aim of all methods was to let the heavy gold sink, while the mud and gravel passed over with the water. Gold dust, gold scales resembling cucumber seeds, and small nuggets the size of peas were usually recovered. One pan, however, provided little as a rule. A rich deposit would yield 25¢ to the pan. Many pans produced "not even the color" of gold. No wonder many miners lost their hope and courage.

The pan, in which water was swirled around and over the side, was used by miners working on their own. Much more mud and gravel could be worked by bigger equipment. The cradle or rocker came in various sizes. Many were crude wooden contraptions rather like a baby's cradle. The mud and gravel were dug out and thrown in the cradle, water was added, and the mixture rocked to help the gold settle while the mud and gravel escaped with the water.

One problem arose from the gold in dust or powder form. Much could be lost, since the particles stuck to bits of mud or air bubbles and simply floated away. This was prevented in part by the use of mercury or quicksilver to form an amalgam, in which gold, "wetted" by the mercury, became brittle, lost its color, and then sank.

The mercury was simply put into the pan, rocker, or other device, and the whole mess sloshed around. The amalgam and the remaining mercury were later taken out and poured through heavy, close-sewn canvas, or better yet, chamois, a soft leather. The free mercury filtered in drops that were caught in a vessel. The amalgam in the chamois was squeezed dry by twisting the corners. The hard compact lump of amalgam was then heated in a retort and the mercury driven off, sometimes to be recovered by cooling en route to a container. In other cases, the amalgam would be heated, sometimes in an old pan, and the mercury boiled off, or allowed to escape into the air. This could be dangerous, especially to the eyes.

Curiously, California was already famous for its rich mercury mines. The ore was cinnabar, a red mineral, mainly mercury. The most famous mine was called New Almadén, after the Almadén mercury mine in Spain. It was situated a few miles from the coast, about midway between San Francisco and Monterey, in a mountain ridge.

The cradle or rocker could be worked by from two to four miners, depending on its size. More mud and gravel was processed per man this way, but even so, some deposits were not worth working. Bigger and more expensive equipment was needed. This conflicted with the free-enterprise spirit of the forty-niners, quite apart from their lack of capital.

Early on, mining was particularly rewarding in the bars of rivers, where the gravel was shallow, often not more than two or three feet deep. A successful miner had "struck his pile," but usually barren rock or gravel was found. Deposits scantily supplied with water, or those deep underground, were avoided at first. Later, they had to be worked. Desperate miners, called jumpers, would sometimes force out the operator of a good deposit, an activity called claim jumping. Others formed partnerships. A contraption known as a tom or long tom made its appearance. This was a wooden channel, or trough, fitted, as was the rocker or cradle, with riffles that caught the gold as the material moved through it. The tom could be extended by tapering the end to fit it into another segment, hence the long tom. Mercury also was used as in the pan or rocker. The rocking motion of the cradle was thus abandoned in favor of a longer piece of equipment that was more efficient, more easily operated, and could handle much more mud and gravel than the larger rockers operated by four men.

The long tom, of course, like the rocker and the pan, had to be cleaned out to recover the gold. That became quite a problem with sluices, or long races or boxes that could run to several hundred feet. Much gold, with the mercury, was left overnight in the sluices. Thieving the amalgam was known as sluice robbing.

Building and operating such equipment were both expensive and hard work. Some miners preferred to let nature do the job. A stream would be diverted over a digging, making a form of sluice in the earth. This technique duplicated the way the original gold discovery had been made at Sutter's Mill.

The immense amount of material put through these various types of equipment meant that the mud and gravel itself got scarce. Mass-production methods had to be used. Hence the introduction around 1852 of hydraulicking, or using water under pressure, to break up thick beds of gravel found on hillsides. Much later came dredging, as in clearing harbors and rivers.

All these methods were forms of placer mining. The other major method, lode mining, is the underground mining common for other minerals, metals, and ores. It is sometimes known as vein mining, since the valuable ore often is found in thin veins that run through the rock like veins in one's arm. In California, this meant, as elsewhere, digging shafts and tunnels to bring out the gold-bearing rock. Individual miners would sometimes try their luck digging their own holes in a hillside, the encampment being known as coyote diggings. A hillside could become covered with these holes, each containing a miner during working hours. Any unusual noise could bring the miners to the surface, each bobbing out of his hole and staring around. The effect was particularly intriguing, since native Americans often wore red shirts and looked like so many red rabbits wondering what all the commotion was about.

The centuries-old mercury or amalgamation process of recovering gold wasted much gold. The cyanide process was introduced in South Africa in 1890 and made for much higher yields. Fortunately, this method was not available in California in the gold rush. Heaven knows what would have happened if the forty-niners had started messing around with cyanide. Dealing with vaporized mercury was dangerous enough.

In California, if the gold-bearing earth was not already like so much mud in water, it had to be crushed. This particularly applied to gold-bearing quartz. Equipment known as an *arrastra* was used, later being replaced by huge stamping mills.

Gold is clearly not recovered easily, except by the fortunate who pick up a nugget that nature somehow has overlooked. That these nuggets can weigh pounds and be almost too heavy to lift is proved by those that have been found.

Gold is scarce and has long been used as a store of value in coinage and monetary matters. Many nations now object to the use of gold in international finance. The process of reducing gold's importance in monetary affairs is known as the demonetization of gold.

The gold standard, or the linking of international currencies to gold, was first put into practice by Great Britain in 1821. Until then, the principal metal was silver. Other nations used a system known as bimetallism, in which gold and silver had a fixed ratio of exchange, usually 16 or 16½ times in favor of gold.

That figure is itself significant. In 3100 B.C., in ancient Egypt, gold was valued at only 2½ times the value of silver. Since 1821, gold has appreciated even much further than 16½ to 1 in silver terms, an indication that gold is ever more popular and desirable. Other nations, such as the United States, France, and Germany, joined Britain on the gold standard in the 1870s. Currencies are no longer on the gold standard, but gold is still favored in some lands as a means of protecting personal wealth, even settling international transactions.

Today, much of the gold produced is used in jewelry. Industry, especially those plants using electrical and electronic circuits, value the high electrical conductivity of gold (71 percent that of copper), while the chemical industry appreciates gold's resistance to corrosion. Gold also is used in dentistry and in medicine, especially for the treatment of arthritis.

The word "karat," as used in 18-karat gold, is the same as "carat" used in weighing diamonds, as in a 10-carat gem. The word represents the Roman *siliqua*, as $1/24$ the golden solidus of Constantine, or $1/6$ ounce. Pure gold is 24-karat, representing the golden solidus. Metal containing only 50 percent gold is thus 12-karat. The use of the word "karat" for gold fineness is giving way to the percentage method. Thus 12-karat gold may be stamped 50 (percent). Originally, 144 carats (6×24) made an ounce, roughly the same as today.

GLOSSARY

alluvial   Relates to alluvium, the sediments laid down in river beds, flood plains, and estuaries.

amalgam   Here used as the combination of mercury and gold.

arrastra   Machine for crushing rock.

bar   Here used as a mass of sand, gravel, or alluvium deposited by a river.

batea   A wooden bowl with ridges, used for panning gold.

bench diggings   Mining on narrow ledges along hillsides or in large bars.

board-sluice   Long wooden trough, used with plentiful water.

Californio   Native-born Californian of Spanish-Mexican ancestry.

carat   A unit of weight used in gems but deriving from the same source as "karat," used to describe the fineness of gold.

cinnabar   The red ore of mercury (quicksilver).

claim   The portion of mining ground held by a miner.

claim jumping   Forcing a miner from his claim.

color   A reference to gold.

coyote diggings   An area used for coyoting.

coyoting   Digging your own hole in hard rock in the search for gold.

cradle   The rocker, similar to a child's cradle, used to process or rock pay dirt, or gold-bearing material.

cyanide   A process for extracting gold from powdered rock introduced much later in the South African goldfields.

dredging   Mass recovery of alluvium, used much later in California.

dry diggings   A former wet diggings that is now away from water.

Ducks   Refers here to ex-convicts from Australia.

electrum   Gold with more than 15 percent silver.

flume   Originally, an open ditch lined with heavy boards. Later, iron pipe was used.

fool's gold   Pyrite, yellow sulfide of iron.

free mining   A system under which a miner is free to stake his claim.

gold   Heavy yellow metal usually containing small amounts of other metals, notably silver.

ground sluice   The use of the ground itself to form a sluice for washing pay dirt.

Hounds   Refers here to ruffians who troubled San Francisco.

hydraulicking   The use of water under pressure to break up gold-bearing deposits.

jumper   A person who jumps or steals a claim.

jumping   The act of stealing a claim.

karat   Used to denote the fineness of gold. Pure gold is 24-karat. The word is just a different spelling of the word carat, used in weighing gems.

lode   Used here as a vein of gold-bearing mineral in rock. The word derives from the verb to lead. Miners followed the lode, or lead.

long tom   Long movable trough used for washing pay dirt.

Manifest Destiny   Concept that the United States was manifestly destined to dominate the North American continent.

mercury   Metal known as quicksilver, liquid at normal temperatures.

Mother Lode   A specific limited area in the gold-bearing district, often used to describe the whole gold-mining region.

open mining   Same as free mining.

pan   Simple instrument like an ordinary pan but about a foot in diameter and six inches high, with sloping sides.

panning   Using the pan.

pay dirt   The name given to gold-bearing substances.

placer   An alluvial deposit.

pyrite   Fool's gold, yellow sulfide of iron.

quartz   The mineral silica, or silicon dioxide, often associated with gold in California and elsewhere.

quicksilver machine   A cumbersome, outsized cradle which used mercury to absorb the fine gold that otherwise might escape.

red earth   The red mineral cinnabar.

rocker   The cradle.

seeing the elephant   An old American expression meaning having seen too much, all, or enough.

silver   White metal often found in gold.

sluice   Used variously, but generally meaning a long trough or ditch for collecting gold. Sometimes, a string of tapered sluice boxes.

sluice robbing   Stealing amalgam from a sluice.

striking his pile   Finding a pile of pay dirt.

tom   Same as long tom.

vein   An occurrence of ore running through rock.

vigilante   Citizen enforcing the law, but without legal authority.

wet diggings   A placer or alluvial deposit with running water.

ADDITIONAL READING

Boericke, William F. *Prospecting and Operating Small Gold Placers*. New York: John Wiley & Sons, 1966.

Buffum, E. Gould. *Six Months in the Gold Mines*. Los Angeles: The Ward Ritchie Press, 1959.

Caughey, John Walton. *Gold Is the Cornerstone*. Berkeley: University of California Press, 1948.

Clappe, Louise Amelia Knapp (Smith). *The Shirley Letters from the California Mines 1851–1852*. New York: Alfred A. Knopf, 1961.

Lewis, Oscar. *Sutter's Fort: Gateway to the Gold Fields*. Englewood Cliffs, N.J.: Prentice-Hall, 1966.

Shinn, Charles Howard. *Mining Camps: A Study in American Frontier Government*. New York: Harper & Row, Publishers, 1965.

Sutherland, C.H.V. *Gold: Its Beauty, Power and Allure*. New York: McGraw-Hill Book Company, 1960.

Vicker, R. *The Realms of Gold*. New York: Charles Scribner's Sons, 1975.

INDEX

Alamo 10
Alaska 101, 116
Allucial mines: *see* Placer mines
Almadén 124
Alvarado, Juan Bautista 20
Amalgamation (gold recovery method) 51
see also Quicksilver
American Journal of Science and Arts 13
American River 1, 28
Arrastra (quartz crusher) 126
Attitudes to gold rush 104-108
Australia 34, 37, 48, 61-62, 71, 74, 79, 81-82, 115
Austrian Empire 6-7
Aztecs 9

Batea (wooden bowl) 123
Beagle (ship) 40
Bear Flag 19, 28
Bimetallism 126
Blacks, American 71-72, 86
see also Slavery
Bolivia 16, 34, 37
Brannan, Samuel 29-30

Brazil 16
Britain 6-7, 16-19, 34, 47, 70-71, 74-75, 81, 86, 96, 104
Bryce, Lord 7

California Star 28-29
Californian 28
Californios 21, 33-34, 55, 68
Camps: *see* Mining communities
Canada 16-18, 48, 96, 117
see also Britain
Cape Horn (route via) 36, 38, 40-42, 69, 80, 114
Chagres (Panama) 38, 41, 45, 80
Chile 31, 40, 48, 56, 61, 69, 70, 81-82, 85
China 7, 34, 37, 47, 72
Chinese 42, 48, 69-71, 86, 114
Chinese food 48
Cinnabar: *see* Quicksilver
Civil War 82, 87
see also Sherman, Wilkes
Claim jumping 124
Clay, Henry 16
Cockneys in California 78
Coloma 1, 23, 25, 28

Color (referring to gold) 51, 54, 123
Colorado 74
Communist Manifesto 7, 81
Covered wagon train (first) 12
Coyote diggings 125
Cradle (gold recovery method) 51, 123-125
Crime: *see* Vigilantism
Cyanide process 125-126

Dana, James Dwight 11, 13, 87
Dana, Richard Henry Jr. 11, 20
"Dark horse" 92
Darwin, Charles 18, 40
Dickens, Charles 74
Discrimination 66-72, 109-113
Donner Party 12-13
Douglas, David 22
Dry diggings 51, 53, 121-122
Ducks: *see* Sydney Ducks

Economist (London) 75
Engels, Friedrich 7, 81
Europe (general conditions in) 6, 7, 9, 37, 75, 99

"Fabulous Forties" 19
Fear caused by gold rush 104-108
Florida 9
Foreign Miners' License Law of 1850 70
Forty-Eighters 32-36, 58
Forty-Niners 33-34, 36, 47-57, 69
Foster, Stephen C. 41-42, 45
France 6-7, 19, 47, 69-71, 78-79, 117
Free mining 34

Galápagos Islands 40
Garibaldi 7
Georgia 56
Germany 6-7, 34, 47, 56, 70-71, 86
Gold
  discovery 1-2, 13

lure 119-127
output 83-87
Gold Standard 75, 81, 104, 126
Golden Ingot Company 79
Guadalupe Hidalgo, Treaty of 10, 23

Hangtown 63-65
Hargraves, Edward Hammond 81
Harte, Bret 74
Hawaii 31, 101-102
Hounds (roughnecks) 61
"Hungry Forties" 6
Hydraulicking 53, 125

Indians, American 13, 20-21, 27, 29, 33-34, 50, 54, 67-68, 70-71, 114
Ireland 6, 34, 47, 71, 86
Italy 6-7, 47

Japan 48, 72
Jones, R. 30
Justice, Administration of 58-65

Keskydees 69
Klondike 74

Latin America 6, 10, 17, 19, 71
Law and order 35, 57-65
Levi's 80
Lincoln, Abraham 92-93, 95-96, 99
Lode mines 34-35, 53, 121-125
Long Tom: *see* Tom
Lopez, Francisco 20-21, 23
Louisiana Purchase 99
Lyman, C. S. 13

Manifest Destiny 14, 17-19, 24, 92-93, 98-103
Marshall, James W. 1-2, 23, 25, 27-28, 55
Marx, Karl 7, 18, 81
Mason, Richard B. 30
Mercury: *see* Quicksilver

134

Mexican Empire: *see* Mexico
Mexican War 1846-1848 5, 10, 12, 16, 27, 68, 80, 92, 94, 114
Mexicans in mines 60, 68-71
Mexico 5-6, 8-13, 15-20, 22-23, 27, 29, 31-34, 48, 55-56, 71, 85, 96
  route via 40
Mining
  claims 34-35
  communities 35, 55-60
  methods (general) 52, 120-126
Mining camps: *see* Mining communities
Monterey garrison 30
Mormons 29
Morning News 17
Mother Lode 60

Napoleon 9
Nevada 74, 82
New Almadén 124
New Helvetia (Sutter's Fort) 12-13, 27-29
New Mexico 56
New Spain 6, 9, 15
New York Herald 31
New Zealand 37, 48, 79, 81-82
Nicaragua (route via) 40
Nichols, John 41
North Carolina 56
Norway 47, 71

"Oh, California" 41
"Oh! Susanna" 41, 45
Old Put: *see* Stone, John A.
Open mining: *see* Free mining
Oregon country 13, 16-18, 31, 67, 94, 99, 116-117
"Oregon fever" 15
Oregon question 16, 96, 116
Oregon Territory 94
Oregon Trail 12, 95
Orientals 71
  see also China; Chinese; Japan
O'Sullivan, John L. 17

Output of gold: *see* Gold (output)
Overland route 37-42

Pacific islands 31, 37, 48
Panama (route via) 37-42, 45, 80, 114
Panama Canal 5, 36, 38
Panning 50-51, 54, 56-57, 123-125
Partnerships, Mining 51-54
Peru 31, 34, 37, 40, 48, 56, 69, 81, 85
Placer mines 34-35, 51, 53, 121-125
Polk, James K. 10, 16-19, 22-23, 30-32, 91-97
Population 32-33, 85-87
Portugal 6, 10, 16-17
Potato famine 6, 47
  see also Ireland
Prices (in California) 49-50, 54
Punch (London) 75-78

Quicksilver 13, 21, 51, 67, 120, 123-126

Racial discrimination: *see* Discrimination
Robinson, David G. 42
Robinson Crusoe's island 40
Rocker (gold recovery method) 51, 54, 123-125
Roosevelt, Franklin D. 96
Routes to California 37-41
  see also Cape Horn; Overland; Panama
Ruelle, Baptiste 21
Russia 7, 47, 56, 116-117

Sacramento 1, 27
  see also New Helvetia
San Francisco 7, 24, 27-33, 35-38, 40-42, 45-46, 49, 57-65, 69, 71, 79, 81, 86, 114, 117
Scandinavians 47, 71
Scott, Winfield 13

"Seeing the Elephant" 42-43
Sherman, William T. 30, 87
Sherwood, John I. 42
Slavery (question of) 15-16, 71-72, 97
  see also Blacks
Sluice boxes 51, 125
Songs of the gold rush 41-45, 74
South Africa 74, 115
South America: *see* Latin America
Soviet Union 19
  see also Alaska; Russia
Spain 6, 9-10, 15-17, 19-20, 34
Spanish-Americans 69-71
  see also Chile; Peru
Stone, John A. (Old Put) 42
Strauss, Levi 80
"Struck his pile" 124
Sutter, John A. 1, 11-13, 23, 25-29, 55
Sutter's Fort: *see* New Helvetia
Sweden 47, 71
Switzerland 27, 47
  see also New Helvetia

Sydney Ducks 62

Teams, Mining 52
Texas 6, 9-10, 12, 15-18, 94, 100
Times (London) 8, 75
Tom (gold recovery method) 51, 124-125
Twain, Mark 74

United States Magazine and Democratic Review 17

Vein mining: *see* Lode mines
Vigilantism 58-66

Wages 48-49, 54
Wales 56
Washington, George 94, 96
Waterloo, Battle of 9
Wet diggings 51, 53, 121-122
White-collar route 40
Wilkes, Charles 11, 87

Year of Revolution (1848) 6